QUIVERTREE
PUBLICATIONS

reuben cooks

food is time travel

Flavours are personal. You have to cook with your own palate and everyone's memories are different, so you can't plan this experience, but often it just happens... things come together and create a time warp – Reuben Riffel

Food is time travel.

Food is time travel. It is a vehicle that has the power, through smells, tastes, colours and shapes, to take us back to another time. Food evokes memory and emotion like nothing else, especially when these are connected to your childhood and your mother's cooking. It's almost like regression therapy. Creating dishes that evoke nostalgia through flavour has always been important to me. Food should awaken your senses in both a physical and a metaphysical way.

Flavours are personal. You have to cook with your own palate and everyone's memories are different, so you can't plan this experience, but often it just happens... things come together and create a time warp. I once cooked black bean soup for a group of Mexican tourists. It wasn't something I had grown up with, but I used the flavours I thought would work, adding sweet balsamic vinegar. They each had two bowls before their main course, and came back to the restaurant every day for the rest of their holiday.

Someone once called my restaurant menu 'unstructured', which in a way was a compliment. We compile the menu at the last minute and it includes whatever I find fresh that day and whatever I feel like eating. Being a good cook means being open to the opportunities presented by fresh, unexpected produce, and knowing what to do with it. Broadly, my advice is to buy what's in season, and don't decide what you're making until you know what good stuff is available.

My food cravings are usually triggered by memories of my mother's cooking. Mothers have an instinct for what you need to eat when you're cold, or tired, or really hungry. It's about complete comfort. If people have one such experience, the place where they had it will become their favourite restaurant. The best chefs are those who 'listen' to their own palate, which allows them instinctively to sense what the majority of people want. Emotions are inextricably tied up with food – making something that everyone loves involves not only luck and coincidence, but sensitivity and understanding.

For me, the smell of peaches drying in the sun, the taste of bottled grapes, the smell of hot gravel when working the soil with my grandfather, all these take me back to my childhood, a very happy place.

As a chef you have to be constantly changing and progressing; you can't keep making the same things. But even though my menus are influenced by other places and cultures and experiences, many dishes remain redolent with memories of my youth and family.

This book is dedicated to my family for all their hard work, their love, loyalty and strength. They were – and still are – keystones of their community. The taste and flavour of everything they have given me will always be with me.

First stop, Franschhoek.

When we were older and naughty, she kept us all in line with a leather strap, which may have helped me when I became a chef, because it taught me discipline!

My great-grandparents came to Franschhoek in the late 1800s and the family has lived here ever since. My grandfather was a carpenter who had nine sons and two daughters. Ouma, my grandmother, was the disciplinarian in the family, and no one ever disobeyed her. There were 40 grandchildren in all, and along the way Ouma looked after all of us while our parents were at work. I was born in Ouma's front room and she took care of me during the day from when I was five months old. When we were older and naughty, she kept us all in line with a leather strap, which may have helped me when I became a chef, because it taught me discipline!

I grew up in Groendal, in Oak Street, which used to be a gravel road. Groendal has been kept safe from the invasion of tourist businesses and fancy houses, because people hardly ever sell their homes. When they do it is only to approved buyers from within the community, so in many ways it has retained its character. It was a very close-knit community when I grew up there. The kids would all play together. We'd go to the river and have 'boat races' with bits of wood, and in December we would climb the mountains together to get our Christmas trees. We were always having neighbourhood gatherings, and food was a central part of these.

People grew things in my neighbourhood. There are still fruit trees everywhere. We were all raised on fresh produce picked straight off the land. Growing our own fresh produce has always been a family tradition – I still use the herbs my mother grows at the restaurant, and my father still grows pumpkins, mielies, beans and marrows. There's something about home-grown produce that you don't find in shops. One of my uncles used to store Granny Smith apples under the floorboards of his house. They go yellowish as they age and when you bite into them they have rich pockets of sweetness, like dessert wine. You can't buy apples that taste like that.

Oupa fed his large family by growing vegetables – pumpkins, mielies, beans, potatoes, peas – on his smallholding outside Groendal, among the vineyards. Every day he would walk along the railway line and work on his crops. He raised pigs there, and he had donkeys to pull the cart full of vegetables that he brought home. When the peas were ready there would be a big family outing to harvest and shell them. He had a shed where he hung onions to dry. I loved it in there. It was dark and cool, with beams of sunlight criss-crossing from the holes in the corrugated iron. He would also dry beans, and we had fun when these were ready – you toss big bunches of them in the air until all the dry skins have blown off and you're left with just the beans. We'd keep sacks of beans for winter soup and some would be pickled and bottled, after we had supplied all the neighbours. At home, while Ouma did the cooking, Oupa would sit in his chair on the stoep and peel fruit for us kids.

I use a lot of fruit in my cooking, probably because of its childhood associations. We grew almost every kind of fruit. There was much baking of apples and pears. My mother and Ouma would make jams and preserves, bottling gooseberries, apricots, plums, grapes, wild bramble berries and the tiny, sweet, wild grapes that we called *katballetjies*.

We had a wood-burning stove when I was a child. My ouma still has hers. My father was a builder and my mother worked at restaurants during the day, so the fire in the stove had to be lit and ready for cooking when they got home. Every Friday a local man, Oom Tol, would come round with his truck and deliver wood for the week. My job, when I got home from school, was to chop the wood and carry it in to make the fire.

Ours was a musical family. My ouma still sings in the church choir on Sundays and my uncle plays the organ. Some of my uncles formed a travelling band, The Mascots. They had ordinary jobs during the week, but at weekends they played at dances in Gansbaai and Malmesbury, doing cover versions of rock numbers, mostly Queen. Uncle Dennis could do all Freddie Mercury's mannerisms and copied the hairstyle – he fancied himself as a bit of a rocker. Uncle Tommy played the organ and sang, and Uncle Willie played drums and guitar. My dad was the bouncer. They would all pile into a big old Ford station wagon, and after the gig we'd hear them coming back over the mountain pass, a bit tipsy and still singing. Sometimes they'd stage a performance at my grandparents' house, which was on a big piece of land. We'd spray water on the ground to keep the dust down while people danced, and the whole neighbourhood came along.

Often we don't even realise that many of our preferences in later life – shapes, colours, tastes – come from things we loved as children. There was always an old car in the garden that the kids could play in, and we'd hear my uncles jamming all the time. I love old cars and music because they trigger happy childhood memories. Oom Sampie across the road from us had an old *dikwiel* bicycle and I would go over and help him fix it. I could have been equally happy as a mechanic or a musician, but I didn't have those skills. Luckily for me, another of the arts – cooking – is in my blood.

So many of my memories involve food. One of our last big family outings was to the fishing village of Paternoster on the West Coast. We hired a bus because there were about 40 of us, including kids – but since we'd gone for the cheapest bus, it wasn't in great condition. The first tyre burned out not far from home, near Paarl. My uncles changed it and we kept going, but it was a really hot day so it wasn't long before the rest of the tyres began to disintegrate. We pulled into Vredenburg on smoking wheel rims. I hitchhiked into town and got the police to give me a lift to Paternoster so I could organise a replacement bus. This collected everyone a few hours later and our day only started late in the afternoon, but it was great. The fishermen were pulling in boatloads of crayfish. They took the tails to sell and gave us the heads. We brought home bags full of heads, cooked them in newspaper to filter out the good flavours, and made incredible soup.

There was always too much food,
but my cousins and I would still want pudding,
so my mother made us **roly-poly cake with jam,**
syrup and custard late in the afternoon.
At the same time she would bake a big batch of
soetkoekies, *klapperkoekies* and *gemmerkoekies*
– sweet biscuits, coconut biscuits and ginger biscuits.

On Sundays, the whole extended family would gather at Ouma's house for a huge family lunch, always with three meats. A chicken would be killed and pot-roasted; there would be roast lamb, pumpkin, cauliflower with white sauce, sweet carrots with vanilla, cabbage and a big hearty green-bean stew. Afterwards all the kids would play ball games in the street. There was always too much food, but my cousins and I would still want pudding, so my mother would make us roly-poly cake with jam, syrup and custard late in the afternoon. At the same time she would bake a big batch of *soetkoekies*, *klapperkoekies* and *gemmerkoekies* – sweet biscuits, coconut biscuits and ginger biscuits. These were kept in a plastic cake holder, and we'd have them when we came home from school. They were supposed to last the week, but of course they never did! My mother has always made the best pumpkin cakes I've ever tasted. She still makes them as a treat for the restaurant staff.

On certain Sundays our tailor, Mr Daniels, would arrive from the Bo-Kaap in his big white Mercedes. He had a driver, so he'd be sitting in the back seat like a king, wearing a fez with the tassel arranged perfectly. He came to measure us for suits – everyone had their suits tailor-made then.

These rituals have disappeared nowadays, but there are so many tastes and flavours that, for me, evoke the spirit of those times. The way of life may be almost gone, but the food remains.

Next stop, the world.

My cooking has been influenced a great deal by the flavours of my childhood and enhanced by food experiences from all over the world. I love strong, robust flavours. I believe that you should taste the essence of what you're eating from the very first mouthful. The most important thing about cooking is to use the best produce available. I was lucky in that I learned from chefs who were happy to share their secrets with me. Some cooks jealously guard their methods, but I'm not one of those. My family taught me generosity, and I'm always happy to give a recipe to anyone who asks for it.

I didn't always want to be a chef. After I matriculated in 1992, I worked for my father in the building trade, but I hated that and left. I wanted to join the navy, but I didn't have the right contacts, so I was hanging around the house, playing dominoes and cooking for my friends. I'd make spaghetti and French toast, and my mother would be really irritated when she came home and found I'd used up all her spices. I said I'd work if she found me a job, so she called Chamonix restaurant, where she worked in the kitchen, and they employed me as a waiter. I had developed a taste for restaurant food when I was very young, because she'd bring us leftovers from the weekend buffet. I loved the roast lamb and the potato gratin, but my favourites were the trifle and crème caramel.

Working at Chamonix was no picnic, however. My high school in Paarl had been pretty lax when it came to discipline, and here suddenly everyone was instructing me and shouting at me. Plus my mother was always telling me how to behave and how to speak to people. I loved the food, but I hated the job and the fact that

I couldn't spend time with my friends, because I was working whenever they were out having fun. My mother threatened to throw me out of the house if I didn't stick it out, so I stayed.

Then I started helping in the kitchen, which I preferred. Fresh out of school, I hadn't had much contact with anyone outside of my own community, so suddenly dealing with the public, with people from all backgrounds and countries, was quite stressful. Being behind the scenes was better than being up front and dealing with people, but I still hated the long hours and the work. That was where I learned how tough the restaurant business is.

It gave me the confidence that I could cook, the way musicians who play by ear learn to play music – I learnt to do it on my own just by watching and by tasting.

My first mentor, Christophe Dehosse, was a brilliant classical chef and a hard-core disciplinarian. The very first thing he taught me was how to debone and tie a leg of lamb. I progressed to shucking oysters, cooking mussels and vegetables, making sauces – all the essential basics. When I was on duty at the Sunday buffet, carving the lamb and making sure it was properly cooked, I met some of the people who are now regular customers at my own restaurant.

Christophe was replaced by another great chef, Richard Carstens, who became my second mentor. He was a creative eccentric, and I effectively became his *sous chef*, doing all the vegetables and sauces. Under Richard I learnt the production cycle of cooking, which required a great deal of efficiency, since we had a very small plating area and served up to 50 diners at a time. One day Richard didn't come to work and I had to take over. I was sending my own food out and receiving compliments, and that got me hooked.

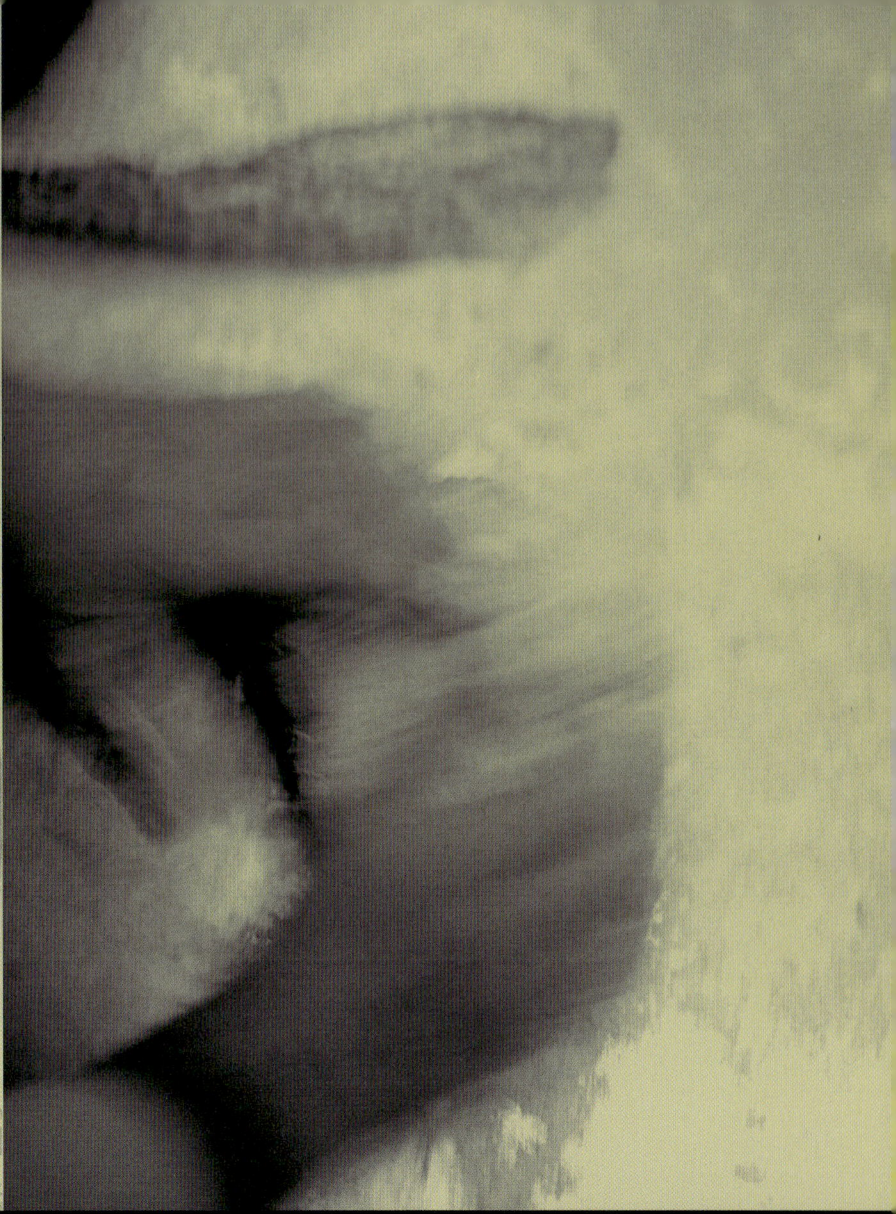

Richard never came back and I was suddenly head chef. It gave me the confidence that I could cook, the way musicians who play by ear learn to play music – I learnt to do it on my own just by watching and by tasting. I'd had excellent chefs as my teachers, so I knew how things were supposed to taste. I knew I had the palate for it, but I needed to learn the methodology. I decided to make this my career. It was a conscious mind shift – once I'd decided that this was what I was going to do, I was far more committed and interested, and enjoyed it a lot more.

The owner of Chamonix was pleased with me and took me on a trip to the Portuguese islands of Bombom and São Tomé, off the west coast of Africa. This was my first trip abroad and I discovered new foods, such as strong chilli sauces. I still use some of these in certain dishes, although they have to be toned down a bit for South African palates. Then, two months after returning, I left Chamonix to gain wider experience as a *sous chef*.

The restaurants I worked at after Chamonix were about volume rather than quality, and although I learnt a lot I knew that wasn't my thing. Richard Carstens had in the meantime become head chef at Monneaux, a fine Franschhoek restaurant, and invited me to work there. I became his second in command, and when he left I took over as executive chef. I was very inexperienced, but I was determined to put good food on plates. At Monneaux I was given the freedom to play, and that's where I established myself as a chef. We used to make raw salmon carpaccio there long before the sushi trend arrived in South Africa.

This was the time when I began to be curious about food and cooking trends. I began buying all the gourmet magazines and journals (and I still do) to see what was happening. In food, as in fashion, trends trickle down from *haute cuisine* – the *haute couture* of food – to the supermarket and the table at home. A great deal of my inspiration comes from soaking up ideas from other countries and other chefs. You can't reinvent food, but you can try different combinations and textures. I believe in using other people's influences along the way to discovering what really works for you. Your personal favourite flavours are a combination of what you grew up with and what you learn by way of new discoveries in the science of food. It's a bit like making wine – everyone uses the same ingredients, and by and large the same method, but everyone's wine contains a personal trademark, and you can taste it.

While I was at Monneaux, an American guest invited me to participate in the food festival in Chesapeake Bay. This was my second trip abroad, and in the States I learnt to love oysters, soft-shelled crab, catfish, scallops and crab cakes. Travel is essential for chefs, I think. You need to broaden your palate, to be inspired by new tastes. You can't make the best things if you haven't tasted the best things.

My next international sojourn was longer-term. A couple who were regular visitors to Monneaux when on holiday told me they were opening a restaurant in Cambridge in the United Kingdom, and offered me the job as chef. When I arrived in Cambridge, the restaurant wasn't finished. Luckily I had some experience in that

Maryké and I returned to South Africa and Reuben's was born. I hadn't ever dreamt of running a restuarant with my name on it, but when the sign went up and I saw my mother's proud face, it was thrilling.

area, so before I could start cooking I helped finish the roofing, plumbing and tiling. The restaurant – Bruno's Brasserie – was in a back street in a fairly dodgy area, between a pawn shop and a kebab shop and across the road from the Salvation Army. Patrick, the owner, wanted to serve ordinary, affordable food, but I dug my heels in and said if we made extraordinary food, it wouldn't matter where we were or what it cost, people would come. And they did. We became famous for our seafood, and I am still good friends with many of the people who were our suppliers. In England I also discovered a multitude of small suppliers – people who don't put a huge mark-up on what they sell, but are nevertheless dedicated to providing the best.

My influences during that era were far wider than just British. I learnt to make my favourite Sichuan chicken soup from a Chinese scullery hand, and an Irishman taught me about colcannon, which is always on the menu at Reuben's. At the time when I was working in Cambridge, fancy fusion cooking was all the rage. To counteract this I started serving simple things, such as fish cakes with chips and Béarnaise sauce. Sometimes you have to go away to realise how much you value the things you grew up with.

The years I spent in Cambridge were happy and I would have taken over the restaurant as my own, but when Marc Kent and Tim Rands from Boekenhoutskloof wine farm came and offered me the opportunity to run my own place in my own home town, I couldn't resist. Maryké and I returned to South Africa and Reuben's was born. I hadn't ever dreamt of running a restaurant with my name on it, but when the sign went up and I saw my mother's proud face, it was thrilling.

There have been a lot of awards and fanfare since Reuben's opened, but cooking isn't about being in the spotlight. The publicity doesn't change the fact that, for me, it's all about food. Everyone enjoys different things at different times, and it is a constant challenge to keep innovating and to keep pleasing people's palates.

My family has been integral to the success of Reuben's – my mother still bakes all our bread early every morning. As for pastry, my aunt Rebecca was pastry chef at Le Quartier Francais, another fine Franschhoek restaurant. She was there when it was still called 1688 and was owned by the mayor. She could do anything with pastry and was one of my mentors. Sadly she has now passed. Aunt Rebecca maintained, as do I, that the best puff pastry is made with margarine, not butter. Pastry is the one thing in cooking that is absolute science. In other areas you can experiment, but with pastry you have to stick rigidly to the rules or it's a disaster.

Rebecca took food very seriously. Even after she stopped working, she'd come to Reuben's to taste things and she'd criticise anything she didn't like. It annoyed me at the time, but I know she did it because she cared. Good cooking has always been an important value in our family, and she wanted me to be the best.

I'm an instinctive chef rather than one who follows rules. When I participate in cook-offs and competitions, where one is required to explain one's methods, I definitely prefer to cook first and

explain afterwards. Cooking involves playing and using your imagination – you can't always explain why you're doing what you're doing. I think this comes from growing up around naturally gifted cooks.

Those who only learn to cook at chef's school can sometimes be a little too regimented. You have to have an open mind in order to be able to experiment and create. When it comes to combining tastes and flavours, smells and shapes, and colours and textures, you never know what new experience might be just around the corner. If that taste has the power to touch people's emotions and awaken their memories, you've hit the jackpot.

Food doesn't have to be fancy and extravagant to be delicious. If you have a really good peach or apricot, you want to retain that taste, so you should do as little as possible to it. Too much messing about with food makes it lose its identity, its essence. It shows a lack of respect for the items you're cooking. I believe in looking for new ways to do things, but simplicity is always the key.

contents

SOUPS

SALADS AND DRESSINGS

MAINS: FISH AND SEAFOOD

MAINS: POULTRY

MAINS: MEAT

starters

Caramelised onion and blue cheese tarts with tomato chutney

Serves 8

4 onions, peeled and very thinly sliced
225ml canola oil
500g puff or shortcrust pastry
185g blue cheese
60g mascarpone
1 egg yolk
100g shredded spinach leaves

Tomato chutney
2 tablespoons vegetable oil
1/2 teaspoon black onion seeds
1 bay leaf
2 dried chillies
500g tomatoes, seeded and chopped
1 1/4 teaspoons mild fresh red chilli powder
200g granulated sugar
1 tablespoon raisins

My development as a chef has gone through various phases. I grew up with a certain kind of food, but went through a transition phase when I entered the restaurant trade – I started cooking only 'sophisticated' things and left out all of the old home staples. Then I gradually returned to these and began combining my family's traditional flavours into 'modern' dishes. This is a recipe that uses modern techniques, but also evokes the essence of my childhood tastes. It has been on the menu at Reuben's from the beginning and I daren't ever take it off because people come back for it again and again.

Preheat the oven to 200°C. Caramelise the onions in the oil until deep golden brown (about 30 minutes). Drain off the excess oil and set aside. Roll the pastry out onto a lightly floured surface to a thickness of 7mm and cut out 8 discs, each 100mm in diameter. Chill in the refrigerator for 30 minutes. Mix the blue cheese, mascarpone and egg yolk together in a bowl. Bake the tarts blind until they are pale brown (about 8 minutes). Divide onions, spinach and cheese mix among the 8 tarts. Return to the oven and bake for a further 10–12 minutes until golden brown. Serve with tomato chutney.

Tomato chutney
Heat the oil and add the onion seeds, bay leaf and chillies. When they crackle, add the tomatoes and cook until soft. Stir in the chilli powder, sugar and raisins and simmer for 15 minutes, until the liquid has almost evaporated and the chutney is glossy.

WINE: Chamonix Chardonnay 2007 – fruity, orange, floral notes, good balanced fruit with integrated oak

Serves 4

1 egg
120ml iced water
3 tablespoons plain flour
1 tablespoon cornflour
Sunflower oil for deep-frying
12 raw headless prawns, shelled
8 scallops or sliced squid tubes
1 avocado, peeled and quartered
6 spring onions
Basil leaves, to garnish
Chopped fresh chillies, to garnish
Sliced red radishes, to garnish

Onion relish
3 cloves garlic, chopped
100g fresh ginger, peeled and chopped
150ml vegetable oil
2 large onions, chopped
5 tablespoons white wine vinegar
3 tablespoons oyster sauce
1/2 cup granulated sugar
4 chillies, chopped
8 spring onions, chopped
7 lime leaves
2 tablespoons Thai fish sauce

Prawn, scallop and avocado tempura with onion relish

This is one of my many Asian-influenced recipes. I discovered along the way that using the best products makes an enormous difference to the final taste of whatever you're cooking. You should always use Kikkoman soy sauce and Thai fish sauce, for instance, as they have a far superior flavour to other brands.

Combine the egg and iced water in a bowl and stir until well mixed. Sift over the flour and cornflour and mix very briefly until just combined. The tempura batter should be slightly runny. If it is too thick, add more water. Heat the oil and test the temperature by dropping a little batter into it: the batter should rise to the surface and brown in 30 seconds. Coat the prawns, scallops, avocado and spring onions in batter and deep-fry in batches until crisp and golden. Remove from oil and drain on kitchen paper. Serve, garnished with basil leaves, chopped chillies and radish slices, with onion relish on the side.

Onion relish
Fry garlic and ginger in vegetable oil until golden. Add the onion and sauté for 10 minutes. Add the vinegar, oyster sauce, sugar, chillies and spring onions and simmer for 30 minutes, stirring continuously. Add the lime leaves and fish sauce and leave to cool for 5 minutes.

WINE: Lammershoek Roulette Blanc 2006 – floral, peach, earth notes, powerful, rich and tasty

Fresh oysters with three salsas

I had my first oyster when working as a waiter at Chamonix and became immediately addicted, but it was on my first visit to the States, at the Chesapeake Food Festival, that I grew to really appreciate them. As with all foods, the key is getting the very best quality oysters. And their taste should be enhanced, not drowned, by whatever sauce or relish you serve with them.

Freshly shucked oysters

Salsa 1
1 tablespoon capers, chopped
2 small spring onions, chopped
1 small garlic clove, peeled and chopped
2 tablespoons olive oil

Salsa 2
1 small red onion, peeled and chopped
2 tablespoons chopped chives
2 tablespoons red wine vinegar
1 teaspoon caster sugar

Salsa 3
2 tablespoons finely diced cucumber
1/2 red chilli, minced
50ml sugar syrup
1 tablespoon Thai fish sauce
1 teaspoon chopped garlic
2 tablespoons lime juice

In three separate bowls, mix ingredients for each salsa together. Serve oysters over ice and present with three salsas.

WINE: Twee Jonge Gezellen Krone Borealis Cuvée Brut 2003 – penetrating vitality and rich, toasty notes

Steamed Saldanha Bay mussels with fresh cream, *gremolata* and white wine

On my visits to the USA I recognised the value of putting the origins of produce on your menu. It gives diners more information and helps them to make a choice if they know where, say, the salmon or the asparagus comes from. I try to do this wherever possible, for example, with the Chalmar beef we use and with the wonderful mussels from Saldanha Bay.

Serves 2

1 cup Sauvignon Blanc
1 clove garlic, peeled and chopped
1 small onion, peeled and chopped
1kg fresh mussels
1 cup fresh cream
Salt and black pepper

Gremolata
1 cup chopped flat-leaf parsley
2 tablespoons chopped anchovies
1 clove garlic, peeled and chopped
Zest of 1 small lemon
½ cup olive oil
Salt and black pepper

Pour the wine into a large pot together with the garlic and onion. Slowly heat until it just begins to boil. Add the mussels to the pot and steam, with the lid on, until they all open (discard any that don't open). Add the cream and gremolata, season with salt and pepper and quickly heat through. Serve in deep bowls with grilled sourdough bread.

Gremolata
In a bowl, mix all the ingredients together.

WINE: Sagila Chenin Blanc 2007 – light fruit richness with tropical and dry grass notes

Serves 2

$^{1}/_{4}$ cup white wine
$^{1}/_{4}$ cup water
1 small onion, peeled and chopped
1 clove garlic, peeled and chopped
20 fresh mussels
Juice of 2 oranges
$^{1}/_{2}$ cup olive oil
1 banana, sliced into rounds
1 orange, peeled and segmented
1 cup flat-leaf parsley leaves
Salt and black pepper

Steamed mussels with banana, orange, flat-leaf parsley and orange and olive oil sauce

This is an unusual sauce for mussels that perfectly complements their texture and uses the combination of sweet fruit and tart citrus flavours that I love. When you buy fresh mussels, make sure their shells are tightly closed, that they smell fresh and that they have good weight when held in your hand.

Place the wine, water, onion and garlic in a small pot. Heat on high until the mixture starts to boil. Reduce the heat and add the mussels. Steam for 2–3 minutes or until all the mussels have opened (discard those that do not open). Remove mussels from their shells and set aside. Strain the cooking liquid and return it to the pot. Add the orange juice and reduce slightly, then add the olive oil and whisk with a hand blender until the sauce is light and frothy. Mix the banana slices with the orange segments and place on the bottom of 2 plates. Spoon the mussels over the banana and orange and pour the sauce over. Scatter chopped parsley over the plates, season and serve.

WINE: Twee Jonge Gezellen Krone Borealis Cuvée Brut 1999 – poised, elegantly balanced, delicate and refined, lightly fruited

Mussel and salmon *laksa*

Serves 4

850ml vegetable stock
280ml coconut milk
Salt and black pepper
20 steamed, shelled mussels
400g salmon, cut into chunks
Juice of 1 lime (about 2 tablespoons)
2 red bird's eye chillies, chopped (optional)
350g rice vermicelli noodles, cooked
1 handful of coriander or basil or mint leaves, to garnish
Onion sprouts, to garnish

Laksa paste
1 tablespoon whole coriander seeds
3 stalks lemon grass
1/2 cup canola oil
1/4 cup picked fresh coriander leaves
1 tablespoon curry powder
1 tablespoon turmeric
6 lime leaves
1/2 cup grated palm sugar
1/2 cup Thai fish sauce
3 green chillies, chopped
3 red chillies, chopped

Heat the stock in a large saucepan. When hot, add the laksa paste. Simmer for a few minutes and add the coconut milk. Continue to simmer for 5 minutes, stirring frequently. Taste and adjust the seasoning. Add the steamed, shelled mussels and simmer for 1 minute. Add the salmon and simmer for 2 minutes. Add the lime juice and chillies, if using. Bring the soup almost to boiling point, cover the pan and turn off the heat. Serve as soon as the noodles are ready. Reheat the rice vermicelli noodles, drain well and transfer to a large bowl. Moisten the noodles with a little of the soup from the seafood pot. Serve the noodles, soup and seafood in 4 large bowls, garnished with herbs and onion sprouts.

Laksa paste
Blend all the ingredients together to make a fine paste.

WINE: Sequillo White 2006 – intense aromas, flavour of stone, fynbos, honeysuckle and a fresh citrus acidity

Seared scallops with ginger, soy sauce and angel-hair pasta

Serves 2

10cm piece fresh ginger, peeled
2 tablespoons Kikkoman soy sauce
2 tablespoons *mirin* (Japanese rice wine)
$^{1}/_{2}$ cup fresh cream
2 nests of angel-hair pasta
1 tablespoon unsalted butter
1 tablespoon canola oil
10 good-sized scallops
Salt and black pepper
100g fine green beans, blanched and shredded
1 tablespoon chopped chives
Fresh chervil, to garnish

Grate the ginger finely and squeeze out the juice. Add the ginger juice to a saucepan together with the soy sauce, *mirin* and cream. Heat the sauce and keep warm. Cook the pasta in boiling salted water, drain and keep warm. Heat the butter and canola oil in a nonstick pan. Season the scallops with salt and pepper and fry on each side to medium rare. They should also be slightly caramelised on the outside. Transfer the scallops to serving plates with pasta and beans. Heat the sauce through, then whisk it and spoon over the scallops. Serve garnished with chives and chervil.

WINE: Rudera Robusto Chenin Blanc 2007 – dried peaches, citrus peel, nuts, rich, tangy flavours

Tuna and salmon tartare with avocado and ginger dressing

I learnt about raw fish when I worked at Monneaux restaurant, where I was given the freedom to experiment despite my inexperience. Sushi wasn't yet a big trend in South Africa, but we made raw salmon carpaccio to see if it would catch on, and people loved it.

Serves 2

100g fresh tuna
100g fresh salmon
Salt
1 small red onion, peeled and finely chopped
1 small chilli, seeded and finely chopped
4 tablespoons olive oil
1 small avocado, peeled, stoned and diced
Juice of 1 lime
2 red radishes
Baby herbs, to garnish
Sliced chillies, to garnish
Salmon-trout roe, to garnish

Ginger dressing
1 tablespoon lime juice
1 tablespoon caster sugar
50g fresh ginger, peeled and roughly chopped
1 tablespoon olive oil
$^1/_3$ cup white wine vinegar
$^1/_3$ cup light soy sauce
Salt

Cut the tuna and salmon into perfect little cubes and season with salt. Mix the fish cubes with the onion, chilli and half of the olive oil. Toss the diced avocado with the lime juice, remaining olive oil and a little salt. Slice the radishes thinly and place in iced water. To serve, mould the avocado, tuna and salmon onto 2 deep plates, spoon the ginger dressing around and garnish with radish slices, baby herbs, sliced chillies and salmon-trout roe.

Ginger dressing
Put the lime juice and caster sugar in a small saucepan and bring to the boil. Remove lime syrup from the heat and leave to cool, then strain through a fine sieve. Purée the ginger in a blender until totally smooth, adding just enough olive oil to blend. Mix in the vinegar, soy sauce and lime syrup. Season with salt to taste.

WINE: Black Oystercatcher White Pearl 2007 – pungent aromas, lemon, capsicum, fresh ginger

Serves 2

2 x 80g packets of sliced raw salmon
Juice of $^{1}/_{2}$ lemon
2 tablespoon Kikkoman soy sauce
2 tablespoons extra virgin olive oil
2 tablespoons sesame oil
1 clove garlic, peeled and crushed
2cm piece fresh ginger, peeled and crushed
2 tablespoons chopped chives
2 tablespoons toasted sesame seeds
2 tablespoons salmon roe

Sesame and olive oil seared salmon

In this dish, drizzling hot oil over the fish gives it a lovely, slightly seared flavour.

Arrange sliced salmon on a plate. Combine the lemon juice and soy sauce and drizzle this over the salmon. Heat the olive and sesame oil together in a pot until smoking hot. Drizzle hot oil over the sliced salmon. Divide the salmon between 2 serving plates. Scatter with garlic, ginger, chives and sesame seeds, top with salmon roe and serve.

WINE: Ataraxia Chardonnay 2007 – bright mineral notes, penetrating lime aromas, tropical flavours

Chilli salt squid with *nuoc cham*

Olive oil has become too glorified in cooking, if you ask me. There is absolutely no need to cook with extra virgin olive oil – it's a waste of money, for one thing, and the taste is too overwhelming for delicate shellfish. If you must cook with olive oil, use the second pressing. Canola or sunflower oil is fine for cooking most things, though good olive oil should be sprinkled over cooked fish and salads.

Serves 8

200g plain flour
4 tablespoons Maldon sea salt
2 tablespoons freshly ground white pepper
4 tablespoons chilli powder
1 litre canola oil for deep-frying
1kg whole squid, cleaned and prepared
Fresh mint leaves, to garnish
Fresh coriander leaves, to garnish
200ml Japanese mayonnaise, to serve
2 limes, quartered, to serve

Nuoc cham
2 long red chillies, seeded and chopped
1 clove garlic, peeled
1 tablespoon palm sugar
2 tablespoons lime juice
3 tablespoons water
3 tablespoons fish sauce
2 tablespoons rice wine vinegar

Combine the flour, salt, pepper and chilli powder in a bowl and mix well. Heat oil in a frying pan or wok (to 180°C if you have a temperature-controlled deep fryer). Roll the squid in the flour mixture until well coated. Shake off the excess flour and place the squid gently in the hot wok or deep fryer. Deep-fry for two minutes and drain on kitchen paper. Garnish each serving of squid with mint and coriander leaves and serve with Japanese mayonnaise, *nuoc cham* and lime quarters (to squeeze over) on the side.

Nuoc cham
In a mortar and pestle, pound the chillies and garlic to a fine paste. Add the palm sugar and stir to blend, then gently stir in the liquids.

WINE: Katbakkies Chenin Blanc 2005 – nutty oak nuances, lime and apple flavours, tingles with sweet-and-sour tension

Serves 6

$^{1}/_{3}$ cup extra virgin olive oil
3 cloves garlic, peeled and finely sliced
1.2kg squid and tentacles, cleaned and sliced into rings
$^{1}/_{3}$ cup small green olives
Black pepper
$^{1}/_{3}$ cup dry white wine
$^{1}/_{2}$ cup Pernod
2 cups orange segments
2 teaspoons dried oregano
1 dried bay leaf
Salt
$^{1}/_{3}$ cup flat-leaf parsley, roughly chopped

Braised squid with orange, Pernod and green olives

Heat the olive oil in a large, heavy-based frying pan over a medium heat. Add the garlic and fry for one minute. Stir in the squid, olives and some black pepper and cook for a further minute. Add the wine and Pernod and bring to the boil. Add the orange segments, oregano and bay leaf and stir to combine. Reduce heat and simmer, covered, for about 45 minutes or until squid is tender. Check seasoning, stir through the parsley and serve.

WINE: Post House Cellar Chenin Blanc 2007 – citrus zest, almonds, roasted fennel, opulent rich palate

Serves 2

1 whole trout, scaled and gutted
Salt and black pepper
2 tablespoons canola oil
1 tablespoon unsalted butter
10 asparagus spears
1 tablespoon salmon roe, to garnish
Apple zest, to garnish (optional)

Apple purée
2 Granny Smith apples, peeled
2 tablespoons water
1/8 cup caster sugar

Orange sauce
Juice of 3 oranges
1/2 cup orange liqueur
1/8 cup caster sugar
1/4 cup extra virgin olive oil

Trout with apple purée, asparagus and orange sauce

Cut the trout into 6 steaks of equal size and season with salt and pepper. Heat the canola oil and unsalted butter in a nonstick pan and fry the trout steaks until golden brown on the outside and pink but cooked on the inside. Blanch the asparagus in a pot of boiling salted water. Spoon apple purée onto 2 serving plates and top with the trout. Heat the orange sauce and whisk vigorously to froth slightly. Spoon this over the fish and scatter the asparagus over and around the plates. Garnish with salmon roe and apple zest (if using).

Apple purée
Core the apples and cut into quarters. Place the apple quarters in a small saucepan with 2 tablespoons water and 1/8 cup caster sugar. Cover the pot with a lid and heat gently on a low heat. When the apple is soft (after about 8–10 minutes), purée it in a food processor, set aside and keep warm.

Orange sauce
In a saucepan, heat the orange juice until it reduces by half. Stir in the orange liqueur, 1/8 cup caster sugar and the olive oil. Set aside.

WINE: De Wetshof Estate Rhine Riesling 2007 – floral, orange-blossom aromas, green apple flavours, pithy grapefruit finish

Serves 2

2 x 80g packets of thinly sliced salmon
10 caper berries, sliced
1 small clove garlic, peeled and minced
1 small red onion, peeled and thinly sliced
1/4 cup extra virgin olive oil
3 tablespoons balsamic syrup
Juice of 1/2 lemon
Baby herbs (chives, baby beetroot leaves, rocket, etc)
Salt and black pepper

Salmon carpaccio with caper berries, red onion, balsamic syrup and olive oil

Arrange the salmon on 2 serving plates and divide the caper berries, garlic and red onion equally between them. Drizzle over the olive oil, balsamic syrup and lemon juice. Garnish with baby herbs and sprinkle with salt and freshly ground black pepper.

WINE: Ataraxia Chardonnay 2007 – bright mineral notes, penetrating lime aromas, tropical flavours

Prawn bisque with prawn Caesar salad

Serves 6

Olive oil and butter for frying
1 carrot, peeled and finely chopped
2 celery stalks, finely chopped
1 leek, white part only, well washed and finely chopped
1 onion, finely chopped
1 medium-sized fennel bulb, trimmed and finely chopped
1 clove garlic, peeled and chopped
1 tablespoon fennel seeds
1 tablespoon coriander seeds
1 star anise
3 tablespoons tomato paste
1kg prawn heads and shells or 500g raw prawns
4 tablespoons brandy
1 cup white wine
4 Roma tomatoes, roughly chopped
1½ litres chicken stock
¼ cup fresh tarragon sprigs
¼ cup fresh thyme sprigs
¼ cup fresh coriander leaves
2 bay leaves
¼ cup fresh flat-leaf parsley leaves
¼ cup fresh basil leaves
Juice of ½ lemon
2 tablespoons cream

Spontaneity is the key word in good cooking – if I have a craving for something on a particular day, I' ll make it and put it on the menu. Whenever I put a special dish, like this prawn bisque, on the menu because the produce is available and I feel like making it, it sells out. My mother used to make a delicious sauce from prawn heads, and that's what inspired this recipe.

Place a little olive oil and butter in a large saucepan on a medium heat. When butter has melted, add carrot, celery, leek, onion, fennel, garlic, fennel seeds, coriander seeds and star anise. Cook, stirring frequently, for 3–4 minutes or until tender; do not allow to brown. Add tomato paste and prawn heads. Pour in 3 tablespoons brandy and set it alight (to burn off the alcohol), then add white wine, tomatoes, chicken stock, tarragon, thyme, coriander and bay leaves. Bring to the boil, then reduce heat and simmer for 50 minutes. Strain stock through a very fine sieve over a large saucepan. Add parsley, basil and lemon juice, then set aside for 15 minutes to allow flavours to infuse. Strain stock again through a fine sieve over a clean saucepan. Reduce over high heat for about 20 minutes – the stock should become thick enough to coat the back of a spoon. Add cream to reduced stock and simmer until the soup is reduced by approximately half again. Stir in the remaining brandy and set aside until ready to serve.

Prawn Caesar salad

Serves 6

1 tablespoon chopped anchovies
½ cup olive oil
2 tablespoons grated Parmesan cheese
200g baby lettuce leaves
3 eggs, boiled and quartered
1 cup sliced Rosa tomatoes
1 cup sourdough croutons
2 red radishes, sliced
12 headless raw baby prawns, peeled and blanched in boiling salted water

Mix together anchovies, olive oil and Parmesan. Combine lettuce, egg, tomatoes, croutons and radishes and drizzle with dressing. Top with blanched prawns and serve alongside the bisque.

WINE: Porcupine Ridge Sauvignon Blanc 2008 – gooseberry and tropical-fruit flavours, fresh and dry with lenghty citrus finish

soups

French onion soup

Serves 6

6 Vidalia or other sweet onions, peeled and sliced into thin strips
60g butter
Salt and black pepper
$^3/_4$ cup sherry
9 cups clear beef stock
24 round slices of sourdough bread
115g goat's milk Brie cheese, cut into thin slices
1 tablespoon chopped fresh chives
1 tablespoon fresh thyme leaves

When the weather is cold and rainy, all I want is a bowl of hot, savoury soup. You'd be surprised how many people feel the same way. I always include a broth when I compile a set menu, because it gives you intense flavour without making you feel too full.

Sweat the onions in the butter in a large saucepan over medium-low heat for 30 minutes or until golden brown. Season with salt and pepper. Deglaze the pan with the sherry and cook for a further 2 minutes. Add the beef stock and simmer for 15 minutes. Season to taste with salt and pepper if necessary. To prepare the croutons, preheat the oven to 180°C. Toast the sourdough bread slices in the oven for 10–12 minutes or until golden brown. Place a slice of Brie on each crouton and slide under the grill until cheese has melted. To serve, ladle soup into shallow bowls. Arrange 4 croutons in each bowl. Sprinkle with chives and thyme, and grind over some black pepper.

WINE: Solms Wijn de Caab Amalie 2006 – peach fruit with hints of honey plus savoury, earthy and mineral touches

Serves 6

6 corn cobs
2 litres chicken stock
1 small leek, finely chopped
1 clove garlic, peeled and crushed
80g salted butter
1 bay leaf
200ml cream
Salt and black pepper
12 headless prawns, peeled
12 scallops
Basil sprigs

Sweetcorn soup with prawns and scallops

Another family favourite, but adding prawns and scallops to this creamy, farm-style soup turns it into something even more special.

Place each corn cob upright on a chopping board and, using a small sharp knife, cut downwards along the cob to remove the kernels. Place the stock in a large saucepan and bring to the boil, then reduce the heat so that it remains warm. Place the leek, garlic and butter in another large saucepan and cook over medium heat, stirring frequently until the leeks are soft and translucent. Add the bay leaf and corn kernels and cook for another 3–4 minutes. Season to taste. Bring the stock back to the boil and add it to the corn mixture. Simmer for 20 minutes until the corn is tender. Add the cream, then remove from heat. Blend until smooth, using a hand blender or food processor, then push through a fine sieve into a large saucepan. Gently reheat the soup over medium heat until warmed through. Add the prawns and scallops and poach slowly for a few minutes until these are cooked. Serve topped with fresh basil sprigs.

WINE: Cederberg Chenin Blanc 2007 – lovely, zesty tropical tones to underlying fruit

Serves 4

1.2 kg mixed fish (white stumpnose, hake, John Dory)
Juice of 1 lemon
Salt and black pepper
1 x 100g fennel bulb
50g leeks (white part only)
50g carrots, peeled
50ml olive oil
4 tomatoes, skinned, seeded and diced
1 tablespoon saffron threads
1 clove garlic, peeled and crushed
120ml dry white wine
450ml fish stock
8 scallops
8 small raw headless prawns
½ cup cream
6 boiled baby potatoes, halved

Parsley-butter toast
50ml Pernod
1 tablespoon chopped fresh mixed herbs
100g unsalted butter
Juice of 1 lemon
¼ cup chopped parsley
Salt and black pepper
1 small clove garlic, minced
4 slices toasted baguette

Bouillabaisse

Most of the fish we had in my youth was dried or salted. We would cook bokkoms (tiny dried fish) on wads of lit newspaper – the skin chars and by the time the newspaper burns out, the fish is cooked, sweet and tender. We also got wonderful smoked snoek from our local shop, Pieter se Visnet. I remember Pieter whenever I find really fresh fish. My simple version of bouillabaisse contains the heart of those flavours and feelings.

Clean the fish, cutting off the heads, tails and fins (use these to make stock) and removing innards. Cut the flesh into 5cm squares and drizzle with lemon juice, salt and pepper. Slice the fennel, carrots and leeks into thin strips. Heat the olive oil in a pot, then sweat the leeks, fennel and carrots in the oil for about 4 minutes, stirring continuously. Add the tomatoes, saffron and garlic, and sauté for 5 more minutes. Add the wine and fish stock and bring to the boil. Reduce to about ¾ of the original volume. Poach the fish, scallops and prawns lightly in the broth until just cooked. Add the cream and baby potatoes and serve with parsley-butter toast.

Parsley-butter toast
Blend all the ingredients except the toasted baguette in a food processor until smooth. Spread on the toasted baguette slices.

WINE: Hidden Valley Sauvignon Blanc 2006 – passion fruit, tropical tones, invigorating juicy flavours

Serves 4

2kg fresh mussels
2 onions, peeled and finely chopped
5 tablespoons olive oil
1 teaspoon masala
1 teaspoon turmeric
½ teaspoon ground cumin
1 teaspoon crushed garlic
1½ litres chicken stock
1 cup crème fraîche
Salt and black pepper
Fresh coriander leaves, to garnish

Curried mussel soup

When I was first exposed to such things as mussels and oysters, I forgot about my family's simple cooking for a while. But as I progressed in confidence and skill, my palate reminded me that the thing I love most, the thing that will always be my favourite, is farm-style food. I had to go away and be deprived of it before I realised how much I'd taken it for granted. So I began to combine the old, familiar flavours with the exciting new ingredients I had discovered, and this dish is an example of this.

Steam fresh mussels in water in a large saucepan for 5 minutes. Remove mussels from liquid and shells, discarding any that did not open, and set aside. In a large saucepan, sauté the onions in the olive oil until soft. Add masala, turmeric, cumin and garlic to the onions and cook for 3 minutes over a low heat. Add the chicken stock and crème fraîche and simmer until reduced by half. Return mussels to soup. Warm through, season to taste and serve garnished with fresh coriander leaves.

WINE: Damarakloof Racetrack Chenin Blanc 2006 – melon and apricot aromas, intense flavours

Serves 4

1 tablespoon groundnut oil
1 onion, peeled and finely chopped
1 clove garlic, peeled and crushed
1.25cm piece fresh ginger, peeled and chopped
350g peeled and diced sweet potato
350g peeled and diced butternut
1 tablespoon chopped lemon grass
$2^1/_4$ cups vegetable stock
$2^1/_4$ cups coconut cream
Salt and black pepper
Juice and zest of 2 limes

Butternut and sweet potato soup with coconut and lemon grass

I don' t use much ordinary cream in my cooking. In many cases I replace it with coconut cream. Coconut is another smell and taste that transports me straight back to my childhood. My mother would toast flaked, dried coconut and then mix this with cream or milk to pour over desserts. In this soup, the coconut balances the flavours of garlic, lime and lemon grass, giving a Thai twist to a traditional recipe.

Heat the oil in a large saucepan and gently fry the onion, garlic and ginger for about 5 minutes until tender. Add the sweet potato, butternut and lemon grass and cook for a further 3 minutes. Add the stock and bring to the boil. Reduce the heat and simmer, covered, for 20 minutes until the vegetables are tender. Cool the soup slightly, then place in a blender and liquidise with half the coconut cream until smooth. Return the soup to the saucepan and stir in the remaining coconut cream. Season and heat through without allowing the soup to boil. Lastly, add the lime juice. Ladle the soup into bowls and garnish with lime zest.

(Note: if you're a chilli fan, green and red chillies also make an attractive garnish for this soup. De-seed a few chillies and cut them into lengthways strips before blanching in boiling salted water.)

WINE: Simonsig Gewürztraminer 2007 – rose-petal aromas, Turkish delight palate

Serves 4

2 cups chicken stock
1 teaspoon salt
700g all-purpose potatoes, peeled and cut into quarters
100g watercress
$^2/_3$ cup milk
2 tablespoons double cream
Freshly grated nutmeg
Salt and black pepper
Salmon roe, to garnish

Poached oysters
200ml water
A few celery leaves
Pinch salt
12 oysters, shucked, liquid reserved

Watercress and potato soup with poached oysters

Bring the stock and salt to the boil and cook the potatoes for 20–25 minutes until tender. Pick the watercress leaves from the stalks and discard the stalks. When the potatoes are cooked, remove them from the stock with a slotted spoon, leaving the stock in the pot. Mash the potatoes in a bowl and set aside. Add the watercress to the stock and simmer gently for 5 minutes. Fish the watercress out of the stock and pulp it, with a little of the liquid, in a blender or liquidiser. Return the blended watercress and the mashed potatoes to the stock and stir well. Add the milk and reheat gently, stirring continuously. Add the cream, a little freshly grated nutmeg and salt and pepper to taste. Simmer gently, without boiling, for 5 minutes. Serve in soup bowls, with poached oysters and garnished with salmon roe.

Poached oysters
Heat water in a small saucepan. Add the celery leaves, salt and oyster liquid and boil gently for about 4 minutes. Reduce the heat, add the oysters and poach for 5 seconds. Gently remove with a slotted spoon.

WINE: Cabrière Estate Pierre Jourdan Blanc de Blancs NV – caramel, cassis notes, biscuit richness

salads and dressings

Pawpaw, melon and mango salad with mixed sprouts, pine nuts and poppy-seed and lime dressing

Serves 4

1 small pawpaw, peeled and cut into small cubes
2 ripe, but not overripe mangoes, peeled and cut into small cubes
1 small head iceberg lettuce, shredded
1 small sweet summer melon, peeled and finely sliced
Fresh watercress leaves, to garnish
Fresh coriander leaves, to garnish
Mixed sprouts, to garnish
Alfalfa sprouts, to garnish
2 tablespoons pine nuts

Poppy-seed and lime dressing
2 tablespoons black poppy seeds
1/2 cup freshly squeezed lime juice
4 tablespoons Thai fish sauce
2 heaped tablespoons caster sugar

This is a perfect summer salad when fruit is in season and sweet – it must have the ripest fruit in order to work properly. It's healthy without being Spartan, and is one of my favourites. I've been doing it for years without changing a thing, which is not usual for me. Whenever I have to do a set menu it's there, and some regulars order it every time they eat at the restaurant.

Mix the pawpaw and mango cubes together. Divide shredded lettuce between 4 serving plates and place pawpaw and mango mix on top. Arrange slices of melon around the sides and top with watercress and coriander leaves. Scatter with sprouts and pine nuts and spoon over some dressing.

Poppy-seed and lime dressing
Mix all ingredients together.

WINE: Thelema Rhine Riesling 2005 – full-flavoured with floral and lime notes

Serves 2

2 figs
1 small head fresh chicory
2 tablespoons olive oil
2 tablespoons raspberry vinegar
1/2 x 100g log goat's cheese, divided into two 25g pieces
2 tablespoons honey
1 teaspoon pink peppercorns
20g walnuts
Salt

Fig salad with goat's cheese, honey, chicory and walnuts

There's a type of wild fig that grows around Franschhoek. It goes yellow when ripe and has a honey-sweet taste. I know where they grow, although no one cultivates them, and pick them whenever they are in season to use in the restaurant. Other figs will do just as well for this recipe.

Break the figs in half. Separate the chicory leaves and wash. Mix the olive oil and raspberry vinegar together, drizzle over the chicory leaves and toss. Divide onto 2 plates, top with the goat's cheese, figs and walnuts, drizzle with honey and season with smashed pink peppercorns and salt.

WINE: Hermanuspietersfontein Sauvignon Blanc 2006 – rich, tropical and fresh with notes of passion fruit

Serves 4

1 mango, peeled and sliced into thin strips
2 tablespoons Thai fish sauce
1 tablespoon sugar
2 grapefruits
Leaves from 1 head iceberg lettuce, washed and broken into rough pieces
8 medium headless prawns, peeled, cleaned and blanched
1 tablespoon fresh dill
1 tablespoon fresh mint leaves
1 tablespoon fresh coriander leaves
3 red shallots, peeled and sliced into fine rounds
3 red onions, peeled and sliced

Chilli-lime dressing
4 small green chillies
3 tablespoons caster sugar
3 tablespoons Thai fish sauce
3 tablespoons rice wine vinegar
4 tablespoons lime juice

Prawn and grapefruit salad with pickled mango and chilli-lime dressing

This salad combines all my favourite things. I love seafood, Asian flavours, pickles, relishes and fruit, especially tart grapefruit. This uses the best of all those flavours. Many people don' t feel like eating salad in winter, but this one is perfect – spicy, tangy and very easy to make.

Place the mango in a bowl, cover with a mixture of the Thai fish sauce and sugar and set aside for a few minutes to pickle slightly. Peel the grapefruits, removing all the pith, then cut out all the segments between the membranes to form little fillets. Break these fillets into smaller pieces. Place the lettuce, grapefruit, prawns, pickled mango, herbs and shallots in a bowl. Pour over the dressing and toss gently. Pile salad onto a plate and garnish with red onion slices.

Chilli-lime dressing
Combine all the dressing ingredients except the lime juice in a saucepan. Boil for 30 seconds, then remove from the heat, allow to cool and add the lime juice.

WINE: Katbakkies Chenin Blanc 2005 – nutty oak nuances, lime and apple flavours, tingles with sweet-and-sour tension

Serves 2

6 baby beetroots, peeled
1 bay leaf
Salt
1 x 100g log goat's milk cheese, cut into 6 slices
2 Rosa tomatoes, sliced
Mixed seeds (sunflower, pumpkin, poppy, linseed, sesame), lightly toasted, to garnish
Baby beetroot leaves, to garnish (optional)

Yellow-pepper essence
1 large yellow bell pepper, cored and chopped
$^1/_2$ cup olive oil
$^1/_4$ cup raspberry vinegar
$^1/_2$ cup water
$^1/_4$ cup caster sugar
Salt

Goat's cheese and beetroot salad with yellow-pepper essence, tomato and toasted seeds

My first experience of beetroot was that of most South African kids – we'd have it cooked and cold-sliced in a salad with vinegar and onions. When I went to New York for a wine festival I stayed at a hotel called The London, and there for the first time I had raw beetroot, served thin-shaved in a marinade, which I loved. When fresh beetroot is newly in season it is possible to get tiny baby beetroot leaves, which are tangy and tender and tasty, and make a wonderful salad garnish.

Place beetroots in a pot, cover with water and add the bay leaf and a few pinches of salt. Bring to the boil and then simmer, covered, for 20 minutes or until beetroot is soft. Remove from the pot and set aside. Place the sliced goat's milk cheese on serving plates. Top with the beetroot and tomato and scatter with toasted seeds. Drizzle the yellow-pepper essence over and around the salad and garnish with baby beetroot leaves.

Yellow-pepper essence
Place chopped peppers and olive oil in a saucepan and cook on low heat for about 5 minutes until oil turns slightly yellow. Add vinegar, water and sugar and continue cooking until the liquid has reduced to half its original volume. Pour into a blender and liquidise until smooth. Season with salt.

WINE: Fairview Viognier 2006 – jasmine and peach-pip perfume partnering savoury oak notes

Serves 4

4 teaspoons olive oil
4 teaspoons balsamic vinegar
4 large black mushrooms
1 x 100g log goat's cheese, cut into 4 pieces
Rocket leaves
Mixed baby salad leaves
1 cooked artichoke heart, quartered
Salt and black pepper

Brown-butter vinaigrette
250g unsalted butter
50g brown sugar
3 tablespoons balsamic vinegar

Marinated black mushroom and artichoke salad with warm goat's cheese and brown-butter vinaigrette

When you're out shopping and you see something you like that may not be there tomorrow, buy it and cook with it immediately. You may not have the chance again. How much you do to food always depends on the quality of your raw materials – the better your ingredients, the less you need to add to them. Using the best fresh produce that is in season is the secret of good cooking.

Preheat the oven to 180°C. Mix the olive oil and 4 teaspoons of balsamic vinegar together to make the mushroom marinade. Thinly slice the mushrooms and roll them in marinade. Warm the portions of goat's cheese in the oven for a minute, until they just begin to melt. Assemble leaves, marinated mushroom slices and an artichoke quarter on each plate. Place the goat's cheese portion on top of this, season to taste and drizzle with the brown-butter vinaigrette.

Brown-butter vinaigrette
Melt the butter on high heat and cook until it takes on a golden colour. Remove from the heat, whisk in the brown sugar, then mix in the balsamic vinegar.

WINE: Solms Wijn de Caab Amalie 2006 – peach fruit with hints of honey plus savoury, earthy and mineral touches

Serves 2

1 x 400ml tin coconut milk
2 skinless free-range chicken breasts
$^1/_2$ mango, peeled and sliced
1 small red onion, peeled and sliced
1 red radish, sliced and kept in iced water
$^1/_2$ small cucumber, seeded and sliced
$^1/_2$ cup bean sprouts, to garnish
$^1/_2$ cup onion sprouts, to garnish

Green chilli and coriander dressing
1 clove garlic, peeled and chopped
1 teaspoon salt
2 green chillies, seeded and chopped
$^1/_2$ cup fresh coriander
2 tablespoons Thai fish sauce
$^1/_4$ cup lime juice
1 tablespoon caster sugar
$^1/_4$ cup olive oil

Coconut-poached chicken salad with mango, sprouts and green chilli and coriander dressing

Heat the coconut milk slowly in a saucepan. Before it begins to boil, add the chicken breasts, ensuring that they are completely covered with coconut milk. Poach slowly for 15 minutes or until chicken is cooked through (cut a slit in one breast to check). Remove from the heat and leave the chicken to cool in the coconut milk. Transfer to a storage container and leave in the refrigerator until ready to serve. Remove the cooled chicken from the coconut milk. Slice the chicken into thin slices. Arrange mango, red onion, radish and cucumber slices on a plate. Top with sliced chicken. Sprinkle over the bean sprouts, top with the dressing and garnish with onion sprouts before serving.

Green chilli and coriander dressing
Pound the garlic, salt, chillies and coriander in a pestle and mortar until it forms a fine paste. Add the fish sauce, lime juice, caster sugar and olive oil and stir through to mix.

WINE: Quoin Rock Sauvignon Blanc 2005 – fine savoury acidity and minerals backing intense gooseberries and lemon grass

Porcini salad with pine nuts, crispy sage and brown butter

Serves 2

2 good-sized fresh porcini mushrooms (wipe off any grit with a dry cloth)
100g unsalted butter
1/4 cup garlic and thyme infused olive oil
8 sage leaves
1/4 cup pine nuts
Salt and black pepper
2 tablespoons balsamic vinegar
Pinch caster sugar
1/4 cup Parmesan cheese shavings, to garnish
Baby cress, to garnish

Garlic and thyme infused olive oil
2 cups extra virgin olive oil
1 clove garlic, peeled
3 sprigs fresh thyme

Slice the porcini into 10mm slices and set aside. Heat 50g butter in a pan, together with one tablespoon of garlic and thyme infused olive oil. Add the sage leaves to the pan and fry over medium heat until they crisp up. Remove sage leaves from pan and place on paper towel to drain. Add the pine nuts to the pan and toast until golden. Remove the pine nuts from the pan, add a little more oil and fry the mushroom slices for about 10 seconds on each side. Season, remove from the pan and keep warm. Add the rest of the butter to the pan and cook for 20 seconds until butter has browned. Add the balsamic vinegar, the rest of the oil, a pinch of caster sugar and some salt and pepper. Serve the porcini with a drizzle of the brown butter and scatter each plate with pine nuts and sage leaves. Garnish with shavings of Parmesan and baby cress.

Garlic and thyme infused olive oil
Pour the olive oil into a saucepan. Crush the garlic clove and add it to the oil together with the thyme. Warm the oil very gently on a low heat for about 10 minutes. Remove from the heat and leave to stand for about an hour to infuse.

WINE: Thelema Chardonnay 2007 – nutty and spicy with creamy lemon notes

Serves 2

1 good-sized avocado
100g baby rocket leaves
2 tablespoons toasted pine nuts
2 tablespoons balsamic syrup
4 tablespoons extra virgin olive oil
$^1/_4$ cup Parmesan cheese shavings, to garnish
Salt and black pepper

Avocado salad with toasted pine nuts, rocket, Parmesan and balsamic syrup

Halve the avocado with a sharp knife and peel the skin off. Cut into 1-centimetre slices and arrange on two serving plates. Scatter the rocket leaves and pine nuts over the avocado. Dress with balsamic syrup and olive oil. Sprinkle over the Parmesan shavings and season with salt and pepper.

WINE: Iona Sauvignon Blanc 2007 – minerally, figgy flavours with fresh natural acidity

Shredded soy-glazed duck salad with chilli dressing and honey

Serves 4

4 duck Marylands (breasts only)
1 litre master stock (see page 208)
Salt
4 tablespoons *kecap manis* (sweet Indonesian soy sauce, available at speciality food stores)
100g equal mix of fresh basil, mint, coriander and mizuna leaves
2 red radishes, thinly sliced
1 small red onion, thinly sliced
50g mixed sprouts
2 tomatoes, cut into quarters
1 cup sliced cucumber
4 tablespoons honey

Chilli dressing
1 garlic clove, peeled and finely chopped
2 red chillies, finely chopped
½ cup red wine vinegar

Preheat the oven to 180°C. Simmer the duck breasts in master stock for 30 minutes. Remove the duck breasts from the stock, place on an oven tray and sprinkle with salt. Roast at 180°C for 30 minutes. Remove from the oven and leave to cool. When the duck is cool enough to handle, pull the meat off the bone and shred lightly. Drizzle a little *kecap manis* over the duck and reheat in the oven. Toss together the herb and salad leaves, radish slices, onion slices, mixed sprouts, tomato slices and cucumber slices. Divide salad between 4 serving plates and top with the warm shredded duck. Spoon chilli dressing over and around the duck, followed by a drizzle of honey.

Chilli dressing
Mix all the ingredients together.

WINE: Boekenhoutskloof Semillon 2005 – balanced citrus fruits, refined charm

Warm lamb salad with yoghurt-mint dressing

Serves 4

150g dry-packed sun-dried tomatoes
400g lamb fillets
1 medium yellow bell pepper
1 red oak-leaf lettuce
1 small red onion, finely sliced
150g baby tomatoes, halved

Yoghurt-mint dressing
1/4 cup low-fat yoghurt
2 tablespoons coarsely chopped fresh mint
1/4 teaspoon ground cumin
2 teaspoons lemon juice

Place sun-dried tomatoes in a heatproof bowl, cover with boiling water and leave to stand for about 5 minutes or until soft. Drain tomatoes and cut in half. Grill or barbecue lamb fillets until browned all over and cooked as desired. Cover lamb and leave to rest for 5 minutes, then slice thinly. Cut the yellow pepper into quarters. Remove and discard the seeds and membranes. Roast under the grill or in a very hot oven, skin-side up, until skin blisters and blackens. Remove from the oven and cover with clingfilm. After about 5 minutes, remove the clingfilm and peel off the skin. Slice into thin strips. Combine lettuce leaves, onion slices, grilled yellow pepper slices, baby tomatoes, sun-dried tomatoes and lamb slices in a large bowl and drizzle with yoghurt-mint dressing.

Yoghurt-mint dressing
Whisk all ingredients together until well combined.

WINE: Chamonix Pinot Noir Reserve 2005 – clean, fresh, pure fruit, earthy notes on red berries

fish and seafood

South Africa's fishing industry is in a perilous state and it's important to know which fish are plentiful and which should not be eaten until their stocks have had a chance to recover from over-fishing. We shouldn't be eating kob (kabeljou), kingklip or Cape salmon, and I don't serve these at the restaurant. There are plenty of alternatives, such as hake, yellowtail, butterfish and monkfish. The Southern African Sustainable Seafood Initiative lists which seafood species are legal and more sustainable consumer choices. Visit www.wwf.org.za/sassi or email sassi@wwf.org.za for information.

Serves 2

1 x 400ml tin coconut milk
2 x 150g angelfish fillets
3 tablespoons *nuoc cham* (see page 62)
2 fresh chillies (1 green and 1 red), seeded and chopped
1 teaspoon chopped fresh ginger
1 teaspoon turmeric
3 tablespoons lime juice
Salt

Pickled cucumber
1 cucumber, halved lengthways and thinly sliced on a mandolin
Juice of 3 limes
1/4 cup caster sugar
2 tablespoons Thai fish sauce
1/4 cup chopped fresh coriander leaves

Angelfish baked in coconut, lime and chilli with pickled cucumber

Because of the food I loved as a child, I like to put sweet and sour tastes together, and I use very little cream, because it wasn' t really part of our cuisine. Coconut milk is about the closest I get to creamy dishes. That balance of sweet and sour tastes is found in many types of Asian cooking, so I find myself drawn to these flavours.

Preheat the oven to 180°C. In an ovenproof pan, simmer coconut milk on medium heat on top of the stove, until it reduces to half its original volume. Add the fish portions, sweet chilli sauce, chopped chillies, ginger, turmeric, lime juice and some salt. Bake at 180°C for 2 minutes or until fish is cooked to your liking. Serve with pickled cucumber and steamed jasmine rice or a crisp salad.

Pickled cucumber
Mix all ingredients together and leave to stand for 5–10 minutes before serving. (Note: this pickle does not keep and must be eaten on the day you make it.)

WINE: Porcupine Ridge Sauvignon Blanc 2008 – gooseberry and tropical-fruit flavours, fresh and dry with lenghty citrus finish

Serves 2

2 x 150g salmon fillets, skin on
Salt and pepper
Canola oil
2 marrow bones, preferably middle bone with soft marrow inside

Port sauce
2 tablespoons canola oil
¼ cup celery, chopped
1 small onion, peeled and roughly chopped
1 garlic clove, peeled and crushed
½ Granny Smith apple, roughly chopped
1 cup good red wine
1 cup port
1 bay leaf
1 sprig fresh thyme
80g unsalted butter

Squash-and-corn ravioli
1 gem squash
½ cup fresh corn kernels
Leaves from 1 sprig fresh thyme
Salt, pepper and grated nutmeg
150g semolina pasta dough (see recipe on page 115)
Beaten egg, for sealing ravioli

Spinach crème
2 cups baby spinach leaves
½ cup cream
Salt and black pepper

Pan-fried salmon with roasted bone marrow, port sauce, squash-and-corn ravioli and spinach crème

Preheat the oven to 120°C. Season the salmon with salt and pepper and rub each fillet all over with a little canola oil. Heat a nonstick pan over medium heat. Place the salmon pieces in the hot pan, skin side down. Fry for about one minute until the skin is browned and crisp. Turn the fish over and quickly sear the other side. Remove fish from the pan and place in a small oven tray, together with the marrow bones. Bake at 120°C for 4–5 minutes. Remove from the oven and season the marrow bones with salt and pepper. Serve the fish with the bone marrow on a plate. Pour hot port sauce over and serve with squash-and-corn ravioli and spinach crème.

Port sauce
Heat the canola oil in a heavy-bottomed pot. Add celery, onion, garlic and apple and cook over medium heat until they begin to caramelise. Add red wine, port, bay leaf and thyme sprig. Cook over medium heat for 20 minutes or until liquid has reduced to less than half its original volume. Strain sauce through a fine sieve and discard solids. Reduce sauce on high heat for another minute. Remove from heat and set aside. Just before serving, heat up the sauce and whisk the butter into it to emulsify.

Squash-and-corn ravioli
Cut gem squash in half and cook in boiling salted water until the inside is soft. Cook the corn in boiling salted water for 1 minute. Scoop the flesh of the squash out and place in a food processor together with the cooked corn kernels, fresh thyme, and salt, pepper and nutmeg to taste. Process until smooth. Roll out the semolina pasta dough using a pasta machine, starting from the number 8 setting, all the way down to the number 2 setting. Cut 8 circles each 70mm in diameter out of the pasta. Place

ro

1 tablespoon of the squash filling in the centre of each pasta circle. Lightly brush the edges of the pasta with egg and cover with another pasta circle. Firmly press the edges of the pasta circles together to seal. Cook the ravioli in boiling salted water for three minutes, or until al dente, then drain.

Spinach crème
Blanch the spinach in boiling salted water for a few seconds and refresh in iced water. Squeeze out all the excess water and keep aside. Boil the cream down to half its original volume. Add spinach, season with salt and pepper and blend in a food processor to a smooth puree.

WINE: Chamonix Pinot Noir Reserve 2005 – clean, fresh, pure fruit, earthy notes on red berries

Pasta dough

Makes 500g

450g fine semolina flour
4 eggs
6 egg yolks
Olive oil

Sieve the flour into a large bowl and make a hollow in the centre. Add the eggs and egg yolks and beat them with a fork. Gradually work the eggs into the flour until you have a soft dough that is easy to knead. Knead the remaining flour into the dough by hand. Add a splash of olive oil for a smooth dough. Wrap the dough in clingfilm and chill for two hours before using.

Serves 2

2 x 180g portions yellowtail
Salt and black pepper
Canola oil
1 clove garlic, peeled and roughly chopped
1 cup flat-leaf parsley
1 red chilli, seeded and chopped
$^1/_2$ cup olive oil
$^1/_4$ preserved lemon, sliced

Crispy potato wedges
2 medium potatoes, peeled and cut into wedges
Canola oil, for deep frying

Grilled yellowtail with crispy potato wedges, preserved lemon, garlic, parsley and chilli

When I was a child, all the kids had to take turns helping Oupa work his land. It always seemed to be my turn; I think I was easily talked into things. When I was hungry, I would eat the rough-skinned lemons from his old trees, skin and all. The skin was thick, white and chewy and the juice was hot from the sun. The taste of preserved lemons and lemon curd takes me right back there.

Heat a griddle pan until extremely hot and preheat the oven to 180°C. Season the fish portions with salt and pepper and coat with a little oil. Grill fish in the hot pan until well marked with strong brown lines. Remove fish from griddle pan, place on a cold baking tray and transfer to the preheated oven. Bake for about $2^1/_2$ minutes or until fish is cooked to your liking. While fish is baking, blend together the garlic, parsley, chilli and olive oil. Add sliced preserved lemon and toss through. Remove fish from the oven, coat with garlic, parsley and chilli dressing and season. Serve with crispy potato wedges.

Crispy potato wedges
Cook the potato wedges gently in salted boiling water until cooked but still firm. They should be soft, but not quite crumbling. Allow to cool. Preheat canola oil in a deep fryer to 190°C. Fry wedges for 5–8 minutes or until golden brown and crisp.

WINE: Black Oystercatcher Sauvignon Blanc 2006 – complex bouquet with cut grass, capsicum, almond, gooseberry flavours

Serves 2

$^1/_4$ cup fresh cream
$^1/_4$ cup full-cream yoghurt
Juice of $^1/_2$ lemon
1 teaspoon chilli powder
1 teaspoon garam masala
1 teaspoon toasted and crushed cumin seeds
1 tablespoon crushed fresh ginger
1 tablespoon crushed fresh garlic
Salt and black pepper
2 x 180g portions yellowtail

Spinach and cumin dhal
$^1/_2$ cup brown lentils or puy lentils, washed and drained
5 cups water
1 teaspoon turmeric
1 teaspoon salt
1 tablespoon melted butter
1 teaspoon cumin seeds
$^1/_4$ cup chopped onion
$^1/_2$ cup chopped tomato
1 cup chopped baby spinach
$^1/_4$ cup chopped coriander

Cucumber relish
$^1/_2$ cucumber, peeled, cored and cut into tiny cubes
1 tablespoon red wine vinegar
Pinch of salt

Lemon froth (optional)
$^1/_2$ cup milk
$^1/_4$ cup cream
Juice of $^1/_2$ lemon

Tandoori yellowtail with spinach and cumin dhal, cucumber relish and lemon froth

Mix together the cream, yoghurt, lemon juice, chilli powder, garam masala, cumin, ginger, garlic, salt and pepper. Coat the fish with the spice mix and leave to marinate for about 10 minutes. Preheat the oven to 200°C. Place a lightly oiled ovenproof pan in the hot oven for about 5 minutes. Remove the hot pan from the oven and place fish portions on this. Cover with all the sauce. Return to the oven and bake for 3 minutes, then turn fish over and bake for another 2–3 minutes. Serve fish on spinach and cumin dhal, topped with cooking sauce and a tablespoon of lemon froth, and accompanied by cucumber relish.

Spinach and cumin dhal
Boil lentils, water, turmeric and salt in a covered pot on a low heat for 20–25 minutes or until tender. In a separate pan, heat the butter. Add the cumin seeds and chopped onion and sauté until brown (about 5–8 minutes). Add tomato and sauté, stirring regularly, for another 5 minutes. Add the cooked lentils to the pan and stir in the chopped spinach and coriander.

Cucumber relish
Mix all the ingredients together.

Lemon froth (optional)
Combine milk, cream and lemon juice in a small saucepan. Heat slowly until the mixture just starts to boil. Remove from the heat, cool slightly and froth with a hand blender.

WINE: Landau du Val Semillon 2006 – waxy character with good fruit and follow-through

Serves 2

1 small aubergine, thinly sliced
Salt and black pepper
1 baby marrow, thinly sliced lengthways
6 Rosa tomatoes
1 cooked artichoke, halved
1 small red bell pepper
2 x 150g tuna steaks
Olive oil

Olive oil, lemon and oregano dressing
1 small clove garlic, peeled and finely chopped
1 teaspoon salt
1 teaspoon oregano, chopped
Juice of 1 lemon
½ cup lemon-infused olive oil

Char-grilled tuna with grilled Italian-style vegetables and olive oil, lemon and oregano dressing

It is absolutely essential to have good sharp knives. I use Japanese knives that are only sharp on one side. These are used for cutting sushi because they do less damage to the cells of the fish or meat, which makes it look better and stay fresher. Whatever knives you use, make sure they are always sharp so you provide the best in freshness, presentation and texture. You can buy lemon-infused olive oil, but it's much easier to make your own. Simply decant the oil into a container with a whole lemon and leave to infuse overnight.

Scatter the slices of aubergine with salt and layer them in a bowl. Stand for 10 minutes so that the salt draws out the bitter juices, then rinse under cold water and pat dry. Heat a griddle pan until extremely hot and grill the vegetables separately until well marked but not burnt. When the whole red pepper is grilled on all sides, wrap it in foil and leave to cool for 10 minutes. When you remove the foil, the skin should come off easily. Peel, cut open, remove the pips and cut the red pepper into strips. Season the tuna steaks with salt and pepper, rub with a bit of oil and grill on high heat in the same pan used for the vegetables for 2 minutes on each side. They should be medium rare. To serve, slice each tuna steak into three strips, top with grilled vegetables and drizzle with dressing.

Olive oil, lemon and oregano dressing
Crush garlic, salt and oregano in a pestle and mortar. Add lemon juice and olive oil and blend together.

WINE: Springfield Wild Yeast Chardonnay 2005 – rich creamy palate, packed with tropical flavour

Serves 2

1 medium trout, cleaned and gutted
Salt and black pepper
1 red chilli, seeded and chopped
Extra virgin olive oil

Cardamom froth
Extra virgin olive oil
1 small onion, chopped
1 stalk celery, washed and finely chopped
1 star anise
1 cardamom pod, crushed
1/2 cup vermouth
1/2 cup white wine
1/2 cup fish stock
1/2 cup cream
Salt and black pepper

Baby carrots
200g baby carrots
1 tablespoon unsalted butter
1 tablespoon chopped chives
1 red radish, sliced thinly
1 clove garlic, crushed
Salt and black pepper

Roasted whole trout with cardamom froth and baby carrots

Trout farmers in the Franschhoek valley raise particularly good fish, so I use these all the time. My dream is one day to be able to list Franschhoek origins for all the fresh produce on my menu.

Preheat the oven to 200°C. Using a sharp knife, cut diagonal slits, about 10cm apart, into the fish on both sides. Rub salt, pepper and chilli into the cuts and coat the fish with olive oil. Place the fish on a baking tray and bake at 200°C for 10–15 minutes to cook. Remove the fish from the oven, place it on a serving plate and top with the baby carrot mixture and cardamom froth.

Cardamom froth
Heat a little olive oil in a saucepan. Add the onion, celery, star anise and cardamom. Sweat the onion for a minute without allowing it to brown. Deglaze the pot with vermouth and reduce until the mixture is almost syrupy. Add the wine and fish stock, cook for another 5 minutes, then add cream. When the sauce starts to boil, remove from the heat and strain through a fine sieve. Return sauce to a clean pot, season and keep warm. When ready to serve, froth the sauce with a stick blender or whisk.

Baby carrots
Blanch the carrots in salted boiling water until soft but not overcooked. In a pan, heat the butter with the chives, radish slices and garlic. Toss the carrots through this mixture, season and keep warm.

WINE: Glenwood Estate Vignerons Selection Chardonnay 2006 – toasted nut flavours with oak and hints of lime

Roasted squid and prawns with Spanish onions, leeks, parsley and Pernod

Serves 6

360g small squid tubes
Extra virgin olive oil
2 Spanish onions, cut lengthways into 2cm wedges
2 large leeks, white part only, cut into 1cm rounds
12 large raw headless prawns, peeled and deveined, with tails intact
1/3 cup verjuice
1/4 cup Pernod
1/2 cup coarsely chopped flat-leaf parsley
50g cold unsalted butter, cut into small cubes

Preheat the oven to 200°C. Clean squid tubes, then cut down one side and open out so that they lie flat. Using a small, sharp knife, score the inside surface of each squid tube in a criss-cross pattern, then cut into 6cm squares. Heat a little extra virgin olive oil in a frying pan over high heat, add onions and leeks and cook over medium heat, stirring occasionally, until just tender. Remove from pan. Pour a little extra virgin olive oil into a large, heavy-based, ovenproof frying pan or heavy-based roasting pan and place in oven at 220°C until oil is very hot. Remove the pan from the oven, add the verjuice, Pernod, prawns and squid and return the pan to the oven. Roast for 4–5 minutes until the prawns and squid are almost cooked. Remove pan from oven, add parsley and butter and season to taste, then stir until butter is incorporated into sauce. Divide squid and prawn mixture among 6 warmed, deep bowls, and serve with a little sauce drizzled over.

WINE: Hazendal Chenin Blanc Wooded 2006 – subtle oak with vanilla, herb, honey and lime flavours

poultry

Baby chicken with rosemary and lemon

This dish is similar to one I used to love at a restaurant in Stellenbosch called Decameron. They would never give me the recipe, so I tried endless variations until I got it to taste the way I wanted it to.

Serves 2

2 x 400g baby chickens
2 cloves garlic, peeled and chopped
1/2 cup white wine
1/4 cup balsamic vinegar
1 preserved lemon, roughly chopped
1/4 cup olive oil
A few fresh rosemary sprigs
2 red chillies, seeded and sliced lengthways
Salt and black pepper

Preheat the oven to 250°C. Place each chicken on a 30x30cm piece of baking paper and into a roasting tray. Bring the paper up along the sides of the chickens and coat with equally divided portions of the garlic, white wine, balsamic vinegar, preserved lemon, olive oil, rosemary and chillies. Season and enclose the chickens in the paper to form 2 parcels. Roast at 250°C for 35–40 minutes.

WINE: Tokara Walker Bay Sauvignon Blanc 2005 – gooseberry and lemon grass flavours; lovely verve, agility and weight

Grilled quail with grape, mascarpone and tarragon stuffing and couscous

In the Cambridge food market, I once bought a wild duck, something I'd never tasted before. I cooked it with orange, cinnamon and spices, served it with my mother's sweet potatoes, and it was a huge success. My quail is similar, and it's one of the signature dishes at Reuben's. I love Moroccan flavours, and have adapted them to suit the subtler taste of quail.

Serves 4

100g green grapes, halved
100g red grapes, halved
3 tablespoons mascarpone
2 tablespoons fresh tarragon
2 cloves garlic, peeled and chopped
4 deboned quails
Salt and black pepper
3 tablespoons oyster sauce
2 large red bell peppers
Mixed fresh herbs, to garnish

Couscous
150g couscous
Skinned, seeded and chopped tomato from 3 medium sized tomatoes
2 tablespoons chopped fresh coriander
4 teaspoons ground coriander
3 tablespoons extra virgin olive oil
Salt and black pepper

Dressing
100ml olive oil
80ml raspberry vinegar
50g red grapes, halved
50g green grapes, halved
Caster sugar, to taste
1 tablespoon chopped fresh tarragon

Preheat the oven to 210°C. Combine the grapes, mascarpone, tarragon and chopped garlic. Divide the stuffing in four and stuff each bird. Secure the stuffing by using toothpicks to close the cavities. Season and brush with oyster sauce. Place on oven tray and roast for 15–20 minutes. Remove from the oven and keep warm. Place the red peppers under a hot grill, turning occasionally and allowing the skin to blister. After about 8 minutes, remove the peppers and wrap them in foil for 10–15 minutes. Remove from foil wrapping, seed and remove the skin from the peppers and slice into strips. To serve, spoon the couscous on a plate. Top with the quail and roasted bell pepper strips. Spoon the dressing over and around the quail. Garnish with fresh herbs.

Couscous
Place the raw couscous in a medium-sized pot or heatproof bowl and add the boiling water a little at a time, stirring constantly with a fork. When cooked, add the tomato, fresh coriander, ground coriander and olive oil. Season to taste and set aside.

Dressing
For the dressing, whisk the olive oil and raspberry vinegar together, then add the grapes, caster sugar and tarragon.

WINE: Chamonix Pinot Noir Reserve 2005 – clean, fresh, pure fruit, earthy notes on red berries

Stuffed guinea fowl with white tomato sauce and green olives

Serves 2

1 plump guinea fowl
1 egg
4 cloves garlic, peeled and chopped
Salt and black pepper
1 cup cream
$^1/_4$ cup chopped celery
$^1/_4$ cup chopped onion
$^1/_4$ cup chopped leek
$^1/_4$ cup peeled and chopped carrot
1 cup white wine (Sauvignon Blanc)
5 tomatoes, chopped
2 cups water
$^1/_4$ cup fresh tarragon leaves
1 teaspoon chopped preserved lemon
$^1/_2$ cup green olives

Place the guinea fowl on its back and, using a sharp knife, cut off both the breasts, keeping the wings attached to the breasts. Cut off the legs and chop up the rest of the bones into little pieces. Remove the skin from the legs and carefully cut the meat off the bone. Place all the leg meat in a food processor with the egg, 1 chopped clove of garlic, half the tarragon leaves, some salt and pepper, and a quarter of the cream. Blend together to a chunky consistency. (Don't over-blend; this should not be a smooth purée.) Place in the refrigerator for a few minutes. Place the chopped bones in a pot with the celery, onion, leeks, remaining garlic and chopped carrots and lightly brown. Add the white wine, tomato and 2 cups of water and slowly cook over a low heat for about 1 hour. When the stock has reduced to half its original volume, add the rest of the cream, heat slowly and strain through a fine sieve. Reheat sauce, season and add the remaining tarragon leaves, preserved lemon and green olives. Make a small pocket on the inside of each guinea fowl breast, fill the cavity with the sauce and fold the skin over the stuffing section. Repeat with the other breast. Place breasts in the refrigerator for about 10 minutes. Preheat the oven to 200°C. Season the breasts with salt and pepper and place them on a lightly oiled baking tray. Bake for 10 minutes, then turn breasts over and bake for a further 5–8 minutes. Leave to rest for 1 minute and serve.

WINE: La Motte Pierneef Collection Sauvignon Blanc 2007 – organically grown, asparagus, lime, fennel and mineral flavours

Serves 2

$^1/_4$ cup extra virgin olive oil
1 medium white onion, peeled and chopped
1 clove garlic, peeled and chopped
Heart of celery, washed and finely chopped
3 plum tomatoes, blanched, peeled and chopped
$^1/_2$ cup vermouth
$^1/_4$ cup white wine
4 patty pan squashes
12 headless prawns, de-veined
4 quail breasts
Salt and ground white pepper
Fresh tarragon leaves, to garnish
Fresh flat-leaf parsley, chopped, to garnish

Ragout of prawn and quail with tomato, white wine and tarragon

Heat a little olive oil in a nonstick pan. Add the chopped onion, garlic and celery and slowly cook over a low heat without browning. Add the chopped tomatoes, vermouth and white wine and continue to heat slowly until the liquid has reduced to half its original volume. Remove from the heat and strain through a fine sieve, pressing gently on the solids to get as much of the sauce as possible. In a separate pan, heat more olive oil. Slice the patty pans in half and slowly fry until golden brown. Remove the patty pans and add the quail breasts, skin-side down. Fry on all sides for roughly 2 minutes or until cooked but still a little pink in the centre. Remove the quail breasts and add more olive oil to the hot pan. Fry the prawns for a few minutes, until they turn slightly pink. Add the strained sauce to the prawns. Mix in the quail breasts and patty pans. Season with salt and ground white pepper and garnish with tarragon and parsley.

WINE: La Motte Pierneef Collection Sauvignon Blanc 2007 – organically grown, asparagus, lime, fennel and mineral flavours

Serves 4

1 litre chicken stock
1 cup Kikkoman soy sauce
1 cup brown sugar
4cm piece fresh ginger, peeled and sliced
1 whole clove garlic, peeled
1 cinnamon stick
Zest of one orange
1 star anise
1 whole duck (about 2kg)

Black rice
1 cup glutinous black rice
2½ cups cold water
½ cup coconut cream
¼ cup oyster sauce
1 tablespoon Thai fish sauce
2 teaspoons palm sugar

Pineapple-caramel sauce
½ cup palm sugar
½ cup water
2 red chillies, sliced
2 green chillies, sliced
2 tablespoons crushed pineapple
4 tablespoons Thai fish sauce
Juice of 2 limes

Roast duck with black rice and pineapple-caramel sauce

Duck is my mother's favourite. Whenever I have a chance to cook a meal for her, it's what she requests. This is my secret way of roasting duck. I boil it in flavoured stock first, which infuses it with flavour and helps to eliminate a lot of the fat while keeping the duck tender and succulent.

Heat chicken stock in a pot large enough to fit the duck snugly. Add the soy sauce, brown sugar, ginger, garlic, cinnamon stick, orange zest and star anise. Bring stock to boiling point, then reduce heat and add the duck. (It must be completely submerged in the liquid.) Simmer, uncovered, for 50 minutes. Remove the duck from the liquid and place in the refrigerator on a drying rack, uncovered, until completely cool. Preheat the oven to 160°C. Place the duck in a roasting tray and roast, uncovered, for 3 hours. Remove from the oven and leave to rest before carving. Carve the duck and serve hot portions on top of black rice with pineapple-caramel sauce spooned over and around it.

Black rice
Place rice and water in a pot and slowly cook over medium heat until the rice is al dente. If the rice is still too hard for your taste once the water has all been absorbed, add a little more water and cook for a few minutes more. Add coconut cream, oyster sauce, fish sauce and palm sugar. Stir through and keep warm.

Pineapple-caramel sauce
In a saucepan, slowly bring the palm sugar and water to the boil. Simmer until the mixture starts to caramelise. Add the chillies, pineapple, fish sauce and lime juice and cook slowly for 2 more minutes.

WINE: Hamilton Russell Vineyards Pinot Noir 2005 – pure, perfumed, red berry fruit

meat

Serves 8

2 onions, peeled
1kg minced beef (chuck)
1 tablespoon Worcestershire sauce
Salt and black pepper
$^1/_4$ cup olive oil
8 soft burger buns
8 rocket leaves
3 vine-ripened tomatoes, sliced
100g dill pickles, sliced
Store-bought barbecue sauce

Reuben's deli burger

Finely grate one onion and place in a large bowl with all the mince and Worcestershire sauce. Season with salt and black pepper and mix well. Using your hands, form the mince mixture into 8 patties and refrigerate for 20 minutes. Thinly slice the remaining onion. Heat oil in a large frying pan and fry patties and onion on medium heat, turning patties occasionally, until the onions are soft and the meat is cooked to your taste (about 5 minutes for medium). Cut the burger buns in half and toast the flat, cut sides under the grill. Top with rocket leaves, tomato slices, patties, fried onion and pickles. Spread barbecue sauce on the top halves of the buns and close the burgers. Serve with fries and crispy onion rings.

WINE: Your favourite beer

Serves 2

500g pork belly, whole and bone in
2 cups chicken stock
Peel of 1 orange
1 cup soy sauce
1 small piece fresh ginger, peeled and chopped
1 star anise
1 small cinnamon stick
½ cup sugar
Peanut oil, for roasting
Steamed broccoli, to serve
Lime quarters, to serve

Ginger-caramel sauce
¼ cup palm sugar
¼ cup water
2 red chillies, sliced
2 green chillies, sliced
2 tablespoons crushed ginger
4 tablespoons Thai fish sauce
Juice of 2 limes

Braised pork belly with ginger-caramel sauce

When I was growing up, the slaughtering of one of my oupa's pigs would be the occasion for a family gathering. Everyone in the family would be involved in the preparation of the pork. When I started making pork belly in Cambridge, it wasn't a common dish on restaurant menus. Now everyone seems to be doing it. The one we serve at Reuben's is special, partly because I buy the very best pork from my first boss, chef Christophe Dehosse, who is now a successful small farmer of quality produce.

Preheat the oven to 160°C. Place pork belly in a small oven tray, to fit fairly snugly. Mix together the stock, orange peel, soy sauce, ginger, star anise, cinnamon stick and sugar and stir well. Cover the pork with this mixture and cover the pan with foil. Roast in the oven for about 4 hours. Remove pork from the oven and carefully remove the bones. Transfer the pork to another pan. Place a similar-sized pan on top of this. Top with a brick or a tin weighing about 3kg. Leave in the fridge for 3 hours or until completely cool. Remove the pork from the pan, trim the sides and cut into two serving pieces. Preheat the oven to 180°C. Place the pork pieces, skin-side down, on a roasting tray that has been lightly brushed with a little peanut oil. Roast for 10 minutes on either side until nicely crisped. Remove from the oven and serve with steamed broccoli, ginger-caramel sauce and lime quarters.

Ginger-caramel sauce
In a saucepan, slowly bring the palm sugar and water to the boil. Simmer until the mixture starts to caramelise. Add the chillies, ginger, Thai fish sauce and lime juice and cook slowly for 2 more minutes.

WINE: Vergelegen White 2006 – spicy oak over citrus and ripe tropical hints

Lamb shank Madras with *kachumber* salad

Serves 2

2 lamb shanks
1 teaspoon ground turmeric
1 tablespoon coriander seeds
1 teaspoon cumin seeds
1 teaspoon fennel seeds
2 dried chillies
$^{1}/_{4}$ cup chopped fresh ginger
6 cloves garlic, peeled
4 curry leaves
4 tablespoons peanut oil
2 onions, peeled and sliced
1 x 400ml tin coconut milk
$^{1}/_{2}$ cup water
1 small cinnamon stick
3 black cardamom pods
Salt and black pepper
$^{1}/_{4}$ cup tamarind water
Chopped fresh coriander, to serve

Kachumber salad
6 baby Rosa tomatoes, sliced into quarters
$^{1}/_{2}$ cucumber, peeled, cored and cubed
1 small red onion, peeled and chopped
1 red radish, chopped
2 tablespoons red wine vinegar
1 tablespoon chopped fresh coriander
1 teaspoon garam masala

I always have a curry on the restaurant menu, because someone will feel like it whether it's winter or summer. My mom used to make traditional sambals, such as chopped cucumber, tomato and onion, to which she'd add vinegar and sugar for a more robust taste. In the UK I discovered kachumber, *which is almost the same thing, but with salt, vinegar, crushed cumin and chilli powder. You can also add chopped nuts and radishes for texture and a peppery flavour.*

Rub the lamb shanks with turmeric. Place a small frying pan over low heat and dry-roast the coriander seeds until aromatic. Remove these and dry-roast the cumin seeds, then the fennel seeds and chillies. Set the fennel seeds aside. Using a pestle and mortar, grind the other spices to a fine powder. Add the ginger, garlic and curry leaves and grind to a fine paste. In a large pot, heat the peanut oil over a low heat. Add the lamb shanks and seal them until lightly brown on all sides. Remove shanks. In the same pot, fry the onion until soft. Add the spice paste and cook for a few minutes. Add the shanks, coconut milk and water. Bring to the boil and simmer over medium heat for 10 minutes, or until the liquid has reduced slightly. Add the cinnamon stick, cardamom pods and fennel seeds. Season, cover and cook, partially covered, over medium heat, for 1 hour or until shanks are tender. Add tamarind water and chopped coriander and season to taste. Serve with *kachumber* salad and steamed basmati rice or parathas.

Kachumber salad
Mix all the ingredients together.

WINE: Thokozani CV 2006 – a blend of Chenin Blanc and Viognier with a nose of white peach, honey and yellow apples

Serves 2

8 cloves garlic, peeled and chopped
5cm piece ginger, peeled and roughly chopped
200ml water
3 tablespoons vegetable oil
500g lamb shoulder cubes
2 bay leaves
1 cinnamon stick, about 5cm long
8 green cardamom pods, broken open
10 black peppercorns
10 whole cloves
2 onions, peeled and finely chopped
1 teaspoon ground coriander
2 teaspoons ground cumin
3 teaspoons paprika
½ teaspoon cayenne pepper
1 teaspoon salt
5 tablespoons plain yoghurt
½ teaspoon garam masala
Black sesame seeds, to garnish
Fresh coriander sprigs, to garnish

Lamb rogan josh

This is another favourite winter curry that reminds me of home cooking. I grew up on good, strong curry. An aunt of mine lived in Durban, South Africa's curry capital, and used to send us packages of proper curry spices. There are few things as comforting as a spicy biryani or a rogan josh – I've had many guests comment on how good they feel after ordering these.

Blend the garlic, ginger and few tablespoons of water in a food processor until smooth. Heat the oil in a large, heavy-bottomed saucepan on a high heat. Lightly brown the lamb cubes in batches on all sides. Set lamb cubes aside in a bowl. Return the pan to a low heat. Drop in the bay leaves, cinnamon stick, cardamom pods, peppercorns and cloves and stir together for about 30 seconds. Add the onion and fry for about 5 minutes or until lightly browned. Add the garlic and ginger paste and stir-fry for about 30 seconds before adding the ground coriander, cumin, paprika, cayenne pepper and salt. Stir these in well. The mixture will probably be fairly dry at this point. Add the lamb and juices back into the pan, and it should start to moisten up again. Slowly add the yoghurt, a tablespoon at a time, stirring continuously so that each spoonful is properly combined before you add the next one. Cook for a further 4 minutes, then add the rest of the water and stir to combine. Bring to the boil, then reduce heat, cover and simmer for an hour, or until the lamb is tender and the sauce has reduced to a rich gravy. Lastly, stir in the garam masala. Serve garnished with black sesame seeds and fresh coriander sprigs, with steamed basmati rice and vegetable atchar.

WINE: Landau du Val Semillon 2006 – waxy character with good fruit and follow-through

Lamb koftas in tikka marinade with spiced aubergine, tomato raita and cucumber salad

Serves 4

600g boneless leg of lamb

Tikka marinade
½ cup thick plain yoghurt
½ cup tomato passata
¼ cup olive oil
3 cloves garlic, peeled and crushed
1 tablespoon finely grated ginger
2 teaspoons cayenne pepper
2 teaspoons paprika
1 teaspoon chilli powder
1 teaspoon garam masala
1 teaspoon salt

Spiced aubergine
¾ cup extra virgin olive oil
1 large aubergine, diced into small cubes
1 large onion, peeled and thickly sliced
2 cloves garlic, peeled and thinly sliced
4 small tomatoes, blanched, peeled, seeds removed and coarsely chopped
2 red bird's eye chillies, seeded and dry-roasted
½ teaspoon coriander seeds, dry-roasted
¼ teaspoon aniseed, dry-roasted
Juice of 1 lime
Salt

Tomato raita
1 cup thick plain yoghurt
2 small tomatoes, blanched, peeled, seeds removed and finely chopped
2 tablespoons mint leaves, finely chopped
1 tablespoon extra virgin olive oil
½ teaspoon ground cumin
Salt and black pepper

Cucumber salad
2 Lebanese cucumbers, peeled, seeds removed and cut into 6cm strips
Juice of 1 lime
⅛ teaspoon ground cumin

Combine all tikka marinade ingredients in a bowl and mix well. Cut lamb into 8 pieces (each about 8cmx4cmx2cm) and place in a bowl. Add the marinade, combine, cover with plastic wrap and refrigerate for 4 hours. Preheat the grill to medium heat (or barbecue over a medium fire). Thread 2 pieces of lamb onto each of 4 wood or metal skewers, reserving the marinade. Grill, turning and basting occasionally with marinade, for 6–7 minutes on each side or until cooked through. Serve with spiced aubergine, tomato raita, cucumber salad and flour chapattis.

Spiced aubergine
Heat ½ cup olive oil in a large frying pan over medium heat and sauté aubergine in batches, for 5 minutes or until soft and just golden. Transfer cooked aubergine to a large saucepan. Add the remaining oil to the pan. Sauté onion and garlic for 5 minutes or until soft and just golden. Add onion and garlic to aubergine with tomatoes, chillies, coriander seeds, aniseed and lime juice. Season with salt and simmer over a low heat for 30–40 minutes or until reduced to a sauce consistency. Set aside to cool.

Tomato raita
Combine yoghurt, tomato, mint, oil and cumin in a bowl. Season to taste with sea salt and freshly ground black pepper. Cover with plastic wrap and refrigerate until required.

Cucumber salad
Combine all ingredients in a bowl.

WINE: Chamonix Pinot Noir Reserve 2005 – clean, fresh, pure fruit, earthy notes on red berries

Boiled lamb shank with lamb broth and pesto

Serves 2

2 lamb shanks
2 cups chicken stock
1 cup white wine
2 tablespoons fennel seeds
1 tablespoon whole white peppercorns
1 stalk celery, chopped
1 clove garlic, peeled
1 onion, peeled and sliced
1 bay leaf
2 baby fennel bulbs, roughly chopped
3 baby sweetcorn cobs, roughly chopped
Salt and black pepper

Pesto
1 cup fresh basil leaves
1 small clove garlic, peeled and crushed
4 mint leaves
1/2 cup flat-leaf parsley
1 tablespoon pine nuts
Salt and black pepper
1/4 cup olive oil
3 tablespoons freshly grated Grana Padano Parmesan cheese

I grew up with rich, hearty stews, so later when I discovered the French dish pot au feu, *I fell completely in love with it. What inspired me was that it is a slow-cooked stew, but also has the fresh clean taste of fresh ingredients added just before serving. This way of cooking lamb shanks combines my childhood stews and the French classics.*

Place the shanks in a large, heavy-based saucepan. Cover with chicken stock and white wine. Add fennel seeds, white peppercorns, clove of garlic, celery, onion and bay leaf. Bring to the boil, then reduce heat, loosely cover the pot and simmer for about 1 1/2 hours, depending on the size of the shanks. Remove shanks from the pot. Strain off the solids and keep broth separate. Place the shanks back in the saucepan together with the strained broth, fennel and sweetcorn cobs. Cook gently until vegetables are tender. Season and serve in deep bowls with the broth and vegetables, topped with pesto.

Pesto
In a mortar and pestle, pound the basil, garlic, mint, parsley and pine nuts into a purée. Add the seasoning, olive oil and Grana Padano and mix through.

WINE: Chamonix Pinot Noir Reserve 2005 – clean, fresh, pure fruit, earthy notes on red berries

Springbok *tataki*

Serves 2

180g boneless springbok loin, cleaned and membrane removed
Salt and black pepper
6 tablespoons extra virgin olive oil
1 tablespoon Kikkoman light soy sauce
1 tablespoon honey
1 small clove garlic, peeled and finely chopped
1 teaspoon balsamic vinegar
1 heaped teaspoon Dijon mustard
1 tablespoon lemon juice
1 egg yolk
1 tablespoon water
1 tablespoon chopped rosemary leaves
Mixed baby herbs, to garnish

When you are searing meat, to keep it tender your pan should be as hot as possible. I prefer not to put any oil in the pan, because that diffuses the heat. Instead I rub the meat lightly with oil, which gives more of a roasted than a fried effect. I don't know why I love rare meat so much – perhaps it is something about the texture of really good meat combined with sharp flavours.

Make a mixture of salt and black pepper and rub this all over the springbok loin, then rub with a little olive oil. Heat a nonstick pan until very hot and quickly sear springbok until lightly brown on all sides, being careful not to burn the meat. Set aside to cool. Mix together the soy sauce, honey, garlic, balsamic vinegar and 1 tablespoon extra virgin olive oil. Set aside. Combine the Dijon mustard, lemon juice, egg yolk, 3 tablespoons olive oil and 1 tablespoon water. Using a hand blender, aerate this mixture until it forms a light froth on top. Set aside. Using a very sharp knife, cut the cooled springbok into thin slices and arrange on a serving platter. Drizzle with the soy and honey dressing. Froth the mustard dressing once more and dot all over the sliced springbok. Garnish with mixed baby herbs.

WINE: Idiom Sangiovese 2004 – elegant, juicy berry fruit with well-integrated tannins

Pan-fried veal liver with colcannon and brown-onion and Marsala gravy

Serves 4

1 cup button mushrooms
Oil or butter for frying
8 pieces thin-sliced streaky bacon
½ cup clarified butter
1kg veal liver, membranes and veins removed, sliced into 1cm thick slices
Salt and black pepper

Colcannon
350g potatoes, scrubbed
225g cabbage, washed and shredded
3 spring onions, trimmed and finely chopped
25ml milk
25g butter
Freshly grated nutmeg
Salt and white pepper

Brown-onion and Marsala gravy
75g butter
2 large onions, peeled and thinly sliced
1 tablespoon flour
⅓ cup Marsala
1 cup beef stock
Salt and black pepper
Worcestershire sauce

My mother made pan-fried liver for me as a child, the most comforting, nourishing thing. Restaurants in South Africa didn't serve it then, perhaps because good liver suppliers were scarce. But when I went to Cambridge there was such excellent liver available that I taught myself to cook it, always simply, and that's still how I serve it. Colcannon is a traditional Irish side dish with a wonderful nutmeg flavour, a constant favourite on my menu.

Fry the mushrooms in a little oil or butter until lightly brown. Set aside. Cook the bacon under a hot grill until crisp. Set aside. When colcannon and gravy are ready, heat the clarified butter in a nonstick pan. Season the liver with salt and black pepper and fry until browned evenly on all sides, for about 30 seconds per side. Toss the mushrooms with the liver. Serve with hot colcannon and brown-onion and Marsala gravy, topped with bacon pieces.

Colcannon
Cook potatoes in boiling salted water until soft, then cool slightly and skin. Mash by pushing through a sieve or food mill. Cook cabbage in boiling salted water until cooked but still crisp, then drain well. Add cabbage to sieved potato with the chopped spring onions, milk and butter. Mix until smooth. Season to taste with grated nutmeg, salt and white pepper.

Brown-onion and Marsala gravy
Melt butter in a pan and cook the onions, covered, over a medium heat until brown and soft. Stir in the flour and cook until slightly browner, then pour in the Marsala and stock and stir. Season with salt, pepper and a drizzle of Worcestershire sauce. Bring to the boil, then reduce heat and simmer for 15 minutes.

WINE: Diemersfontein Pinotage 2007 – campfire smoke, dark fruit, black-pepper flavours

Serves 4

4 x 200g sirloin steaks, trimmed
Salt and black pepper
Oil for grilling

Herb crust
$1/4$ cup chopped fresh tarragon
$1/4$ cup chopped fresh oregano
$1/4$ cup chopped fresh sage
$1/2$ cup chopped fresh flat-leaf parsley
1 cup breadcrumbs
150g unsalted butter
Salt and black pepper

Béarnaise sauce
2 tablespoons white balsamic vinegar
30g onion, finely chopped
10 peppercorns, crushed
4 egg yolks
3 tablespoons cold water
250g clarified butter
Salt and black pepper
3 tablespoons snipped tarragon
2 tablespoons snipped chervil
Juice of $1/2$ lemon

Herb-crusted steak with Béarnaise sauce

At Reuben's we use Chalmar beef, the best you can get in South Africa. If you cook meat perfectly you shouldn't even need a sauce with it. Covering badly cooked meat with good sauce won't fix it. It's such a compliment to a cook to hear someone say, 'That was a good piece of meat.' There's much debate among chefs about whether to season meat before or after cooking. Either way, you are going to lose some moisture during the cooking process. I believe in salting meat (but not fish) just before cooking, because it concentrates the flavour.

Season steaks with salt and black pepper and rub with oil. Grill on a hot grill (or fry in a very hot grilling pan) until done to your preference. Top with herb crust mixture and place in the oven under a hot grill until the crust crisps up. Remove from the oven and leave to rest for a minute, then slice onto serving plates and serve with Béarnaise sauce on the side.

Herb crust
Mix all the ingredients together.

Béarnaise sauce
Combine the vinegar, onion and peppercorns in a saucepan and boil until the liquid is reduced by half. Set aside to cool. When cold, stir in the egg yolks and cold water. Set the pan over a low heat and whisk, gradually increasing the heat. After about 10 minutes the mixture will start to thicken. Turn off the heat and gradually add the butter, whisking continuously, so that the mixture does not separate. Season and stir in tarragon, chervil and lemon juice.

WINE: Reyneke Reserve 2005 – Rhône-style Shiraz from granite soils with clove, aniseed, dark plum and enduring length

Moroccan meatballs with mint, couscous and red-pepper and sultana salsa

Makes about 30 meatballs – serve 4 per person as a main course

115g red lentils
350g lean lamb mince
3 spring onions, finely chopped
2 cloves garlic, finely chopped
1 egg, lightly beaten
1 teaspoon chopped ginger
3 teaspoons ground coriander
1/2 teaspoon freshly grated nutmeg
2 tablespoons freshly chopped mint or
1 tablespoon freshly chopped rosemary
1/2 teaspoon cayenne pepper
1 teaspoon salt
Whites of 2 eggs, lightly beaten
4 tablespoons plain flour
Vegetable oil, for frying
Fresh mint leaves, to garnish
Fresh coriander leaves, to garnish
Finely sliced tomato, to garnish
Finely sliced onion, to garnish

Couscous
1 1/2 cups couscous
2 cups hot chicken stock
2 tablespoons olive oil
Salt and black pepper

Red-pepper and sultana salsa
2 red bell peppers
Olive oil, for roasting
1 medium onion, sliced
1/4 cup white wine
1 teaspoon crushed cumin
1 red chilli, chopped
1 clove garlic, peeled and chopped
1/4 cup sultanas
2 tomatoes, chopped
2 tablespoons honey

Cook the lentils in boiling salted water for 5 minutes, drain and place in a large bowl. Mix in the lamb mince, spring onion, garlic, egg, ginger, coriander, nutmeg, mint or rosemary, cayenne pepper and salt. Knead the mixture for a minute or two. Mould the mix into meatballs about the size of walnuts. Cover and refrigerate for half an hour. Roll the meatballs in egg white and then in flour. Heat oil in a nonstick frying pan and fry the meatballs until they are golden brown and cooked through. Drain on kitchen paper. Serve with couscous and salsa, garnished with fresh mint, coriander, tomato and onion.

Couscous
Put the couscous in a metal bowl. Pour over the hot chicken stock, to cover the couscous. Add a little salt. Seal the bowl with clingfilm and leave to stand for 10 minutes. Remove the clingfilm and break up the couscous with a fork. Stir through the olive oil and season to taste.

Red-pepper and sultana salsa
Preheat the oven to 180°C. Place peppers in a roasting tin and drizzle with olive oil. Roast, uncovered, for about 35 minutes, or until the skin begins to blister and blacken. Turn the peppers once halfway through cooking time. Transfer peppers and pan juices to a bowl, cover with clingfilm and leave to stand for 10 minutes. Drain off juices and reserve for later use. Peel the skin off the peppers, cut them in half and remove the seeds and inner membranes. Roughly chop the flesh and set aside. Braise the onion in the wine until soft, then add the cumin, chilli, garlic, sultanas, tomatoes, honey and chopped red pepper. Simmer slowly until most of the liquid has evaporated.

WINE: Simonsig Frans Malan Reserve 2004 – supple fruit in harmony with lemon acidity

Serves 4

1 sheep's tripe, thoroughly cleaned
4 sheep's trotters, thoroughly cleaned
4 bay leaves
1 tablespoon whole coriander seeds
10 allspice seeds
6 whole cloves
4 cardamom pods
½ cup brown vinegar
½ cup lemon juice
1 tablespoon curry powder
1 tablespoon turmeric
1 tablespoon sugar
1 teaspoon grated fresh ginger
2 cloves garlic, peeled and crushed
1 onion, peeled and finely chopped
5 teaspoons salt
1 tablespoon ground black pepper
Crispy lettuce leaves
12 cornichons (small pickled gherkins)
12 pickled baby onions
2 eggs, soft boiled and halved
1 small red radish, thinly sliced
4 tablespoons extra virgin olive oil
4 teaspoons balsamic syrup

Mayonnaise
1 egg yolk
2 tablespoons white wine vinegar
1 teaspoon mustard
350ml canola oil
Salt and black pepper

Curried brawn with pickle salad and mayonnaise

There's something about the arrival of winter that triggers a longing in me for certain meals. Winter dishes were big in our family – rich, hearty concoctions using vegetables that had been grown in summer and then pickled. This is my mother's recipe, and whenever I make it I wonder why I haven't done so for so long.

In a saucepan, cover the tripe and trotters with water. Bring to the boil, reduce heat and simmer slowly until the meat falls off the bone. Remove all the bones and cut the tripe into smaller pieces. Tie the bay leaves, coriander seeds, allspice seeds, cloves and cardamom pods in a muslin bag and place in the saucepan with the meat. Add the vinegar, lemon juice, curry powder, turmeric, sugar, ginger, garlic, onion, salt and pepper. Simmer slowly for about two hours. Stir frequently to prevent the mixture from sticking to the bottom of the saucepan. Pour into moulds rinsed with cold water and leave to set. Serve brawn sliced on a serving plate with salad leaves, cornichons, pickled onions, boiled eggs, radishes and mayonnaise. Drizzle the olive oil and balsamic syrup over the brawn slices. This is also delicious served with fresh bread.

Mayonnaise
Mix the egg yolk with the vinegar and mustard. Whisk in the oil, gradually at first, then in a thin stream. Keep whisking gently until the mayonnaise thickens. Season with salt and black pepper.

WINE: Paul Cluver Gewürtztraminer 2007 – rose-petal, honeysuckle and lime notes

Serves 2

2 x 500g matured T-bone steaks
2 tablespoons olive oil
Salt and black pepper

Anchovy, garlic and parsley butter
1 bulb garlic
150g unsalted butter, softened slightly
1 cup finely chopped flat-leaf parsley
1 tablespoon chopped fresh rosemary
2 tablespoons good quality anchovies
Juice of $^1/_2$ lemon
Black pepper

T-bone steak with anchovy, garlic and parsley butter

In this recipe the anchovy paste is used as a sauce, but it also works as a marinade for lamb or beef before grilling, roasting or frying. It gives a lovely savoury flavour without needing to add much salt to the meat. Make sure you get the best quality anchovies you can find – it makes a big difference to the taste.

Preheat the oven to 200°C. Rub the T-bones with olive oil and season with salt and pepper. (It is important for the steaks to be at room temperature before cooking.) Heat a griddle pan over high heat until extremely hot. Sear the T-bones in the hot pan for 4 minutes on each side. Transfer the steaks to the oven and roast for 3–4 minutes. Remove the foil from the anchovy butter and cut the butter into 1cm slices. Place a few of these on top of each T-bone and place under a hot grill. Serve as soon as the butter has melted.

Anchovy, garlic and parsley butter
Preheat the oven to 180°C. Roast the whole garlic bulb for about 10 minutes. Remove from the oven, cut across the top and squeeze the soft garlic out of the skins. Place the garlic, butter, parsley, rosemary, anchovies, lemon juice and black pepper in a food processor and blend until the mixture is smooth. Scoop the butter onto a square piece of tin foil and roll foil into a cylinder shape. Refrigerate until needed.

WINE: Boekenhoutskloof Syrah 2005 – pimento spice, layered with dense, tense palate and exhilarating fruit expression

Mustard-glazed ostrich fillet with tomato *smoor*, polenta and butternut crème

Polenta and tomato smoor *is my homage to the South African staple of* pap en sous.

Serves 2

2 x 180g ostrich fillets
Salt and black pepper
1 tablespoon canola oil
2 tablespoons wholegrain mustard

Tomato smoor
2 tablespoons canola oil
1 small onion, peeled and chopped
1 clove garlic, finely chopped
1 small green pepper, seeded and finely chopped
1 x 400g tin Italian whole peeled tomatoes, chopped
2 tablespoons fresh oregano leaves
Salt and black pepper

Polenta
1 cup milk
1/2 cup water
1/2 cup polenta
1 tablespoon grated Parmesan cheese
1 tablespoon unsalted butter
Salt

Butternut crème
2 cups peeled chopped butternut cubes
1/4 cup fresh cream
2 teaspoons honey
1 teaspoon unsalted butter
2 sage leaves
Salt and black pepper

Season ostrich fillets. Heat the oil in a pan and quickly sear the ostrich on all sides. Remove from pan, coat the top of the meat with mustard and set aside. When ready to serve, preheat the oven to 220°C and roast fillets for 7 minutes for medium rare. To serve, mould the smoor onto a serving plate with the butternut crème. Cut ostrich into slices and arrange on the plates with polenta rounds.

Tomato smoor
Heat oil in a pan, add onions, garlic and green pepper and cook over low heat until onions are translucent. Add tomatoes and oregano and simmer on a low heat until mixture thickens. Season.

Polenta
Pour milk and water into a saucepan and heat without allowing it to boil. Add polenta and cook, stirring continuously with a wooden spoon, until it thickens. Remove from the heat and fold in Parmesan, butter and salt. Pour into a small greased baking tray about 30mm deep. Leave to set in the fridge. When set, cut into rounds, heat in a hot oven and sprinkle with more Parmesan.

Butternut crème
Cook butternut in boiling salted water until soft. Remove and keep warm. Pour cream into a saucepan and reduce until it thickens slightly. Add butternut and honey, heat through and purée in a food processor. Heat butter in a small pan and fry sage until leaves are crisp. Add browned butter and sage leaves to the butternut purée and season. Stir well to combine and set aside.

WINE: Boekenhoutskloof The Chocolate Block 2005 – smouldering dark chocolate sheen with spice and ripe berries

Herb-crusted roast rack of lamb with aubergine purée, roast garlic, sage and red wine jus

Serves 2

2 x three-bone racks of lamb, French-cut (ask your butcher to do this)
1 tablespoon olive oil
Salt

Herb crust
$^{1}/_{4}$ cup fresh breadcrumbs
$^{1}/_{4}$ cup fresh parsley, rosemary and thyme leaves, chopped
1 tablespoon wholegrain mustard
1 tablespoon grated Parmesan cheese

Jus
8 cloves garlic, peeled
$^{1}/_{4}$ cup olive oil
8 sage leaves
1 cup good red wine
2 cups chicken stock
1 tablespoon apricot jam
1 tablespoon unsalted butter

Aubergine purée
1 aubergine
1 tablespoon olive oil
Salt and black pepper
$^{1}/_{4}$ cup double cream yoghurt

Preheat the oven to 200°C. Rub the lamb lightly with olive oil and salt. Heat a pan over medium heat and sear the lamb, skin-side down, for 2–3 minutes. Turn over and sear the other side for 1 minute. Place the lamb on a baking tray and coat with the herb crust. Roast for 8–10 minutes for medium rare. Remove the lamb from the oven and allow to rest in a warm place. To serve, spoon some aubergine purée onto a plate. Cut the lamb into three pieces per rack and arrange on the plate. Cover the lamb with the jus and some roast garlic and sage. Serve with hot polenta rounds (see page 166).

Herb crust
Mix all the ingredients together.

Jus
Boil the garlic cloves for about 5 minutes in salted water until soft. Transfer them to a pan, add the olive oil and slowly fry until the garlic cloves are golden brown. Add the sage and fry until the leaves are crisp. Remove sage and garlic from the pan and add the red wine, chicken stock and apricot jam. Reduce the liquid to less than half the original volume and whisk in the butter.

Aubergine purée
Preheat the oven to 200°C. Cut the aubergine in half and cut criss-cross patterns into the white flesh. Rub olive oil and salt into the cuts and place the two aubergine halves on a roasting tray. Roast for 10–15 minutes. Remove from the oven and scoop the flesh out from the skin. Place aubergine pulp in a food processor with the yoghurt and blend until smooth. Season.

WINE: Porcupine Ridge Syrah 2007 – spiced berries, dark fruit, rustic and well-balanced

Serves 2

6 lamb tails
2 cups chicken stock

Red-pepper paste
1 clove garlic, peeled
1 tablespoon anchovies
2 roasted red peppers, peeled, seeded and chopped
1 tablespoon chopped fresh rosemary
1 tablespoon Dijon mustard
Black pepper

Polenta
1 cup milk
$^1/_2$ cup water
$^1/_2$ cup polenta
1 tablespoon grated Parmesan cheese
1 tablespoon unsalted butter
Salt

Lamb tails with polenta and red-pepper paste

In a large pot, cook the lamb tails in chicken stock for $1^1/_2$ hours over medium-low heat or until the meat around the bone starts to soften. Preheat the oven to 200°C. Remove the tails from the stock and transfer to a roasting tray. Roast the tails for 15 minutes or until they start to crisp slightly. Spoon red-pepper paste over the roasted lamb tails and serve with hot polenta.

Red-pepper paste
In a pestle and mortar, pound the garlic and anchovies into a smooth paste. Add the red peppers, rosemary, mustard and some freshly ground black pepper and mix together.

Polenta
Pour milk and water into a saucepan and heat without allowing it to boil. Add polenta and cook, stirring continuously with a wooden spoon, until it thickens. Remove from the heat and fold in Parmesan, butter and salt. Pour into a small greased baking tray about 30mm deep. Leave to set in the fridge. When set, cut into rounds, heat in a hot oven and sprinkle with more Parmesan.

WINE: Boekenhoutskloof The Chocolate Block 2005
– smouldering dark chocolate sheen with spice and ripe berries

pasta and risotto

Serves 6

3 litres light chicken stock
100ml olive oil
40g butter
100g chopped white onion
2 cloves garlic, peeled and finely chopped
500g Arborio rice
1/2 cup vermouth
100g grated Parmesan cheese
Salt and black pepper
Juice of 1/2 lemon

Basic risotto

Stock is the most important ingredient in risotto. A heavy chicken stock makes the risotto too stodgy, so I prefer to use a light stock, which allows the thickening to come from the rice and the butter, without any added gelatine from the stock. One of the secrets of good risotto is to add the stock bit by bit, but to keep the risotto simmering on a medium heat so that the stock is absorbed fairly quickly. If you keep the mixture bubbling away fairly rapidly (without letting it stick to the bottom) you will save your arm as well as your risotto. If you allow the risotto to lie in warm stock for too long, it will overcook and be stodgy.

Bring the chicken stock to the boil and reduce to half its original volume. Keep hot. Heat the olive oil and half the butter in a large heavy-bottomed saucepan over medium heat. Add the onion and garlic and cook for 2 minutes or until onion is translucent, but not brown. Add the rice to the pan, stir and cook over medium heat for two minutes. Add the vermouth and cook until the liquid has all evaporated. Add the boiling chicken stock to the rice mixture, one ladle at a time. Stir continuously with a wooden spoon until the rice has absorbed all the liquid, then add another ladle of stock. Continue until the rice is just cooked, then add the remaining butter, Parmesan, seasoning and lemon juice. Remove from the heat and stir until butter and Parmesan are well incorporated into the risotto. Serve with fried porcini mushrooms, asparagus, or whatever vegetables are in season.

WINE: Scali Blanc 2005 – complex flavour, aromatic, rich texture

Gorgonzola and watercress risotto with toasted pine nuts

Serves 2

4 tablespoons extra virgin olive oil
1 1/2 cups Arborio rice
1/2 medium onion, peeled and finely chopped
1 clove garlic, peeled and finely chopped
1/4 cup vermouth
1/4 cup white wine (Sauvignon Blanc)
3 cups light chicken stock
80g fresh watercress, large stalks removed
3 tablespoons unsalted butter
1/2 cup Gorgonzola cheese, crumbled
60g Grana Padano Parmesan cheese
Freshly grated nutmeg
Salt and black pepper
1/4 cup toasted pine nuts, to garnish
Fresh watercress, to garnish

My ideal restaurant would serve only three main dishes: a meat dish, a fish dish and a risotto. Risotto is all about combining flavours, and the important part is how you get the flavour into the risotto. When using parsley (or watercress), for instance, you don't get enough flavour simply by adding chopped raw herbs at the end – it's best to cook the herbs slightly and blend thoroughly into the rice.

Place a large, heavy-bottomed saucepan on medium heat. Add the olive oil and rice. Sauté the rice lightly over a low heat for a minute, then add the chopped onion and garlic. Stir continuously with a wooden spoon and control the heat to make sure the mixture softens without browning. After 2 minutes, deglaze the pan with the vermouth and continue stirring. Add the white wine after the vermouth has been completely absorbed. Continue stirring. In a separate pot, heat the chicken stock, but do not allow it to boil. Add chicken stock until the rice is just covered and continue stirring. As the stock absorbs, add more, stirring and keeping the risotto on a medium heat. After adding the third ladle of stock, the rice should have swollen significantly. Taste the rice to give you an idea of how long it needs – the rice should be al dente, but not raw. Add one more ladle of stock and reduce by half, so that you have a loose risotto that is still quite moist. Remove the pan from the heat. Add the butter, gorgonzola, freshly grated Grana Padano, freshly grated nutmeg, salt and pepper. Stir slowly to properly incorporate all the ingredients. You should have a creamy-textured risotto. Sprinkle with toasted pine nuts and some fresh watercress.

WINE: Allesverloren Port 2003 – rich dark fruit with hints of caramel and nutty nuances

Serves 6

$^{1}/_{2}$ cup extra virgin olive oil
40g pine nuts
400g fennel, trimmed, washed and sliced
3 onions, peeled and finely chopped
450g white anchovies
40g raisins, soaked in warm water for 10 minutes and drained
500g tagliatelli, cooked and drained
200g grated Grana Padano Parmesan cheese
Salt and black pepper
Fresh fennel fronds, chopped, to garnish (optional)

Tagliatelli with white anchovies, fennel, raisins and pine nuts

The strong taste of fennel and the savoury saltiness of anchovies are perfectly balanced with the rich sweetness of raisins here. Find a supplier who sells really high-quality 'white' anchovies – these have a creamy texture and a much better flavour than the others.

Heat $^{1}/_{4}$ cup olive oil in a large, heavy-based frying pan. Add the pine nuts and fry until light golden. Remove the pine nuts, leaving the oil in the pan. Cook fennel in a large pot of boiling salted water until tender (about 10 minutes). Remove from heat and drain, reserving $^{1}/_{2}$ cup of the fennel cooking water. Add the rest of the olive oil to the pan containing the pine-nut toasting oil. Heat, add the onions and fry over medium heat for 10 minutes or until soft and golden. Add the white anchovies, fennel, pine nuts, raisins, cooked tagliatelli, a little of the fennel cooking liquid and the Parmesan. Toss until warmed through and season. If using, chop fresh fennel fronds and scatter over pasta before serving.

WINE: Terra del Capo Pinot Grigio 2005 – easy drinking with winter melon and green apple interest, balanced freshness

Serves 4

12 ripe plum tomatoes
3 tablespoons extra virgin olive oil
2 cloves garlic, peeled and finely chopped
1 leek, finely chopped
1 red chilli, finely chopped (remove the seeds if you want it milder)
250g tagliolini (or pasta of your choice)
150g raw small prawns or shrimps, headless and cleaned
150g squid or calamari steak, cleaned and sliced
Salt and black pepper
Olive oil, to garnish
Fresh herbs, to garnish

Squid and prawn pasta with tomato and chilli

Score the bottom sides of the tomatoes with a sharp knife and blanch in boiling salted water for 20 seconds. Remove the tomatoes from the water and refresh in a large bowl of ice water. Peel the skins off the tomatoes, cut them into quarters, remove and discard the seeds, and chop finely. Heat the oil in a large saucepan and fry the garlic, leek and chilli on a low heat for 3 minutes. Add the tomatoes and simmer for 10 minutes. Meanwhile, cook the tagliolini in boiling salted water until al dente and drain. Add the pasta to the tomato sauce. Blanch the prawns and squid in boiling salted water for 15 seconds. Add seafood to the pasta and sauce. Season and serve with a drizzle of olive oil and fresh herbs.

WINE: Porcupine Ridge Sauvignon Blanc 2008 – gooseberry and tropical-fruit flavours, fresh and dry with lengthy citrus finish

Serves 2

2 tablespoons olive oil
1 teaspoon chopped garlic
1 small onion, peeled and finely chopped
1 cup carnaroli rice
¼ cup vermouth
¼ cup good Sauvignon Blanc
1 litre light chicken stock, warmed
1 moist fresh vanilla pod
80g unsalted butter
Salt and black pepper
2 tablespoons grated Grana Padano Parmesan cheese
1 leek, rinsed and cut into strips
1 cup raw headless prawns, peeled and cleaned

Prawn risotto with vanilla and leeks

Heat the olive oil in a heavy-based pan. Add the garlic and onion and stir with a wooden spoon for a few seconds. Do not allow the mixture to discolour. Add the rice and reduce heat. Stir the rice for another 1/2 minute, then add the vermouth. Continue stirring. Add the white wine after the vermouth has been absorbed by the rice and continue stirring. Slowly add the chicken stock, ladle by ladle. Be careful that the heat is not too low, or the rice will overcook, but not too high, or the rice will not be able to absorb the liquid properly. Just before the rice is fully cooked, split the vanilla pod, scrape out the seeds and add them to the rice, together with the pod. Add the butter, seasoning and Parmesan to the rice and remove from the heat. Gently stir the risotto to incorporate the butter and Parmesan. Heat some salted water in a pot and blanch the leek strips for about 3–4 minutes until tender. Remove from the water and set aside. In the same water, blanch the prawns for 3–4 minutes until pink and cooked through. Remove the vanilla pod from the risotto, spoon hot risotto into serving bowls, top with warm prawns and scatter with leeks.

WINE: Hamilton Russell Vineyards Chardonnay 2007 – bright fruit, well-balanced with toasted oak

vegetarian

Serves 4

60g butter, plus extra for greasing
20g finely grated Parmesan cheese, plus extra for dusting soufflé dish
1 golden shallot, peeled and finely chopped
35g plain flour
1 cup hot milk
2 teaspoons Dijon mustard
4 egg yolks
Salt and white pepper
75g grated Gruyère cheese
5 egg whites

Apple, fennel and pomegranate salad
1 clove garlic, cut sideways, for rubbing
1 teaspoon Dijon mustard
1 tablespoon sugar
1 tablespoon sherry vinegar
2 red apples, cored and cut into eighths
4 tablespoons pomegranate seeds
1 small fennel bulb, thinly sliced

Gruyère soufflé with apple, fennel and pomegranate salad

White pepper has been neglected since freshly ground black pepper became fashionable, but it's the best thing, as far as I'm concerned, to put on eggs. As for the salad, it was inspired by my grandfather's pomegranate trees.

Butter 4x250ml-capacity ovenproof ceramic dishes and dust with finely grated Parmesan, shaking to remove excess. Make a collar out of a double layer of buttered baking paper and tie this around the top of each dish, buttered side inward, standing about 50mm high. Preheat the oven to 180°C. Melt the butter in a heavy-based saucepan. Add the chopped shallot and cook for 2–3 minutes or until soft. Add the flour and stir continuously for 1–2 minutes. Gradually add the milk, mixing until smooth, then bring to the boil, stirring continuously, and cook for 2–3 minutes or until thick. Remove from the heat. Add the mustard and egg yolks and mix to combine. Season to taste with salt and freshly ground white pepper. Leave to rest for 5 minutes, then stir in the Gruyère.
In a bowl, whisk the egg whites with a pinch of salt until soft peaks form. Fold $^{1}/_{3}$ of the egg whites into the cheese mixture to lighten it, then fold through all the remaining egg whites. Pour the soufflé mixture into the prepared, collared dishes. Bake in a bain-marie for 30–35 minutes or until puffed and golden. Remove the paper collars from the tops of the dishes and serve the soufflés immediately with apple, fennel and pomegranate salad.

Apple, fennel and pomegranate salad
Rub the cut garlic clove around the inside of a salad bowl. Whisk the mustard, sugar and vinegar together in the bowl. Add the apple, pomegranate seeds and fennel and toss to coat.

WINE: Tokara Stellenbosch Chardonnay 2006 – lemon and lime facade, tight, sleek mineral structure, well-integrated toasty oak

Serves 4

2 medium aubergines
Salt and black pepper
Olive oil
2 tins whole peeled tomatoes
1 teaspoon chopped rosemary
1 teaspoon chopped oreganum
1 teaspoon chopped thyme
½ cup extra virgin olive oil
1 clove garlic, peeled and minced
12 green olives
2 medium fresh tomatoes
1 tablespoon sugar syrup
200g ricotta
Basil pesto (see recipe on page 209)

Sugar syrup
20ml water
20g granulated sugar
1 basil leaf

Aubergine parcel with green olives, tomato and ricotta

Slice the aubergines lengthways into ½cm-thick slices. Sprinkle with salt and set aside. Heat a griddle pan until extremely hot. Rub the aubergines with olive oil and grill in batches on both sides until well marked. Place the whole peeled tomatoes in a food processor and pulse until chopped. The mixture can be left quite chunky. Add this with the rosemary, oreganum, thyme, 2 tablespoons olive oil and garlic to a pot and over medium heat, cook tomato pulp down for 20–25 minutes until most watery liquid has evaporated. Remove from the pot and leave to cool. Preheat the oven to 100°C. Remove the pips from the olives, cut them in half and place them in the oven for 40 minutes to dry slightly. Reduce oven temperature to 80°C. Slice the tomatoes into ½cm slices and brush them with a little sugar syrup. Place them on a silicon mat and dry in the oven for 1 hour. Set aside. Preheat the oven to 150°C. Take 4 ovenproof dariole moulds or bowls 10cm in diameter, rub the inside of each mould with a little olive oil and line them with the slices of aubergine, making sure the slices overlap and that there is a 4cm overhang to close the parcels properly. Place 2 tablespoons of the tomato sauce in the bottom of each mould, followed by 50g of ricotta. Using the pieces of aubergine that hang over, close the 4 parcels neatly. Bake at 150°C for 20 minutes. Carefully remove from the oven and unmould parcels onto 4 serving plates. Top with dried olives, dried tomatoes and pesto. Drizzle over the remaining olive oil.

Sugar syrup
Place all ingredients together in a saucepan and cook until the sugar dissolves. Remove from the heat and cool.

WINE: Porcupine Ridge Sauvignon Blanc 2008 – gooseberry and tropical-fruit flavours, fresh and dry with lenghty citrus finish

desserts

Serves 2

2 cups water
2 cups sugar
Seeds from $^1/_2$ moist, fresh vanilla pod
1 lime, sliced
2 firm peaches
2 plums
Raspberries, to garnish
Fresh mint leaves, to garnish

Passion fruit and tequila syrup
Pulp of 4 passion fruits
1 tablespoon tequila
$^1/_4$ cup caster sugar

Poached peach and plum with passion fruit and tequila syrup

Put the water, sugar, vanilla seeds amd lime slices in a saucepan and bring to the boil. Cut a slit across the bottoms of the peaches and plums. Place the fruit in the poaching liquid, reduce heat and poach slowly for 10 minutes. Remove the fruit from the syrup and leave to cool. When the peaches and plums are cool enough too handle, peel the skin off, starting at the bottom where you scored the fruit. Serve peaches and plums with passion fruit and tequila syrup and a couple of lime slices from the poaching liquid. Scatter with a few raspberries and fresh mint leaves.

Passion fruit and tequila syrup
Combine all the ingredients in a saucepan, bring slowly to the boil and simmer slowly for 3 minutes or until sugar dissolves completely. Set aside to cool.

WINE: Simonsig Vin de Liza Noble Late Harvest 2006 – apricot earthy tones, minerally rich

Muscat *crème brûlée* with plum ice cream

Makes 15 portions in individual ramekins

1.4 litres cream
Seeds scraped from 2 moist, fresh vanilla pods
150g caster sugar
16 egg yolks
300ml hanepoot wine (muscadel)
About 8 teaspoons caster sugar
Preserved grapes, to serve
Berries, to garnish
Fresh mint leaves, to garnish

Plum ice cream
300ml milk
Seeds scraped from 1 moist, fresh vanilla pod
100g sugar
2 eggs
2 egg yolks
200ml cream
200ml plum purée

Our house was always full of fruit, summer and winter, because my mother and grandmother make all sorts of jams and preserves. Muscadel reminds me of the taste of bottled grapes, which are my mother's speciality.

Preheat the oven to 135°C. In a saucepan, scald the cream with the vanilla. Cream 150g caster sugar with the egg yolks and hanepoot wine. Whisk the scalded cream into this mixture. Strain the mixture and pour it into 15 ramekins. Bake in a bain-marie for 30 minutes or until set. Allow to cool slightly. Coat the top of the custard in each ramekin with about ½ teaspoon of caster sugar and caramelise with a blow torch. Serve *crème brûlée* with plum ice cream and preserved grapes. Garnish with berries and a sprig of mint.

Plum ice cream
Bring milk, vanilla and sugar to the boil. Meanwhile, combine the eggs, egg yolks and cream. Whisk this mixture into the boiling milk mixture, stirring constantly, until it begins to thicken. Strain and leave to cool for as long as possible – ideally, leave it to mature overnight in the refrigerator. Mix in the plum purée and churn in an ice-cream maker to freeze.

WINE: Nuy White Muscadel 2003 – spicy grape aromas, signature mint and iced tea flavours

Grapefruit and tequila *granita* with almond *tuiles*

Serves 3

100g sugar
150ml water
Zest of 1 grapefruit
2 cups strained freshly squeezed grapefruit juice
75ml tequila

Almond or vanilla tuiles
250g egg whites
250g icing sugar
250g cake flour
1 teaspoon almond or vanilla essence

Passion fruit syrup
300g caster sugar
100ml water
250ml passion fruit juice
Pulp of 6 fresh passion fruit

I came up with this granita *while participating in a cook-off. It's a great palate-cleanser, has a delicious bite and has since become a favourite dessert that can be made the day before serving. If you prefer a less sharp flavour, use orange zest and juice instead of grapefruit.*

Bring the sugar, water and zest to the boil in a saucepan. Add the grapefruit juice, stir in and then add the tequila. Remove from the heat, cool, and freeze for 5 hours. Break up the ice crystals with a fork and freeze for a further 5 hours. Serve the *granita* in the *tuile* baskets and garnish with poached soft fruit, citrus segments, fresh berries or passion fruit syrup.

Almond or vanilla tuiles
Preheat the oven to 160°C. Combine all the ingredients and whisk well. Spread teaspoonfuls on a greased baking tray and bake for about 12 minutes, until golden brown. Either allow the biscuits to cool and crisp up as is, or form the dough into small baskets while still warm and pliable, then leave to set.

Passion fruit syrup
Bring the caster sugar and water to the boil in a stainless-steel saucepan and cook without stirring over a high heat until it becomes a pale caramel. Add the passion fruit juice, then reduce the heat and simmer for 10 minutes. Remove the pan from heat and stir in the pulp from the passion fruit. Pour the syrup into a cold stainless-steel bowl to stop the cooking process. Allow it to cool completely before using or refrigerating. The syrup keeps for about a month.

WINE: Stony Brook Annie's Wine 2003 – peach and apricot notes with floral undertones

Raspberry and white chocolate sundae

Serves 2

1 cup whipped cream
100g roasted almonds
100g white chocolate, chopped into tiny pieces
250g fresh raspberries

White chocolate mousse
50g sugar
45ml water
2 egg yolks
180ml cream
25ml milk
100g white chocolate

Raspberry coulis
250g raspberries
4 tablespoons lemon syrup

To assemble, place a layer of whipped cream at the bottom of each of 2 broad dessert glasses. Follow with a layer of roasted almonds, a sprinkle of chopped white chocolate, a layer of white chocolate mousse and a layer of raspberry coulis. Serve as is, or top with fresh raspberries and drizzle with passion fruit syrup (see page 197).

White chocolate mousse
Heat sugar and water slowly in a saucepan, stirring until a light syrup is formed. Remove from the heat. Meanwhile, whisk the egg yolks until pale. Gradually whisk the warm syrup into the egg yolks. Continue whisking till the mixture thickens. In a separate bowl, whip the cream and milk together until thick but not stiff. Melt the chocolate in a bowl over simmering water. Whisk a little cream mix into the melted chocolate, then fold in the rest of the cream and the egg-yolk mixture, and place the mousse in the refrigerator to chill.

Raspberry coulis
Purée raspberries and lemon syrup together and pass through a fine sieve.

WINE: Boekenhoutskloof Noble Late Harvest 2004 – vanilla-scented fruit, fresh finish cuts lushness of caramel core

Serves 6

700g rhubarb stalks, washed and chopped
300g brown sugar
Seeds scraped from 2 moist, fresh vanilla pods
Juice of 1 orange
Juice of 1 lemon

Brown sugar pastry cases
100g soft butter
100g brown sugar
2 eggs
270g flour, plus extra for dusting

Italian meringue
1/2 cup white caster sugar
1/4 cup golden caster sugar
1/4 cup water
2 egg whites

Rhubarb tarts

Rinse the rhubarb in a colander and transfer to a heavy-bottomed saucepan. Add brown sugar, vanilla seeds and juices, and stir over a medium heat until the sugar dissolves. Increase heat and bring this mixture to the boil, then reduce heat to medium again and simmer for 12–15 minutes or until the rhubarb is soft and the liquid is reduced. Set aside until required. To assemble, preheat the grill. Spoon warm rhubarb mixture into prepared pastry cases and set aside. Spoon meringue over the rhubarb and place tarts under the hot grill for 2–3 minutes or until meringue is golden.

Brown sugar pastry cases
Process butter with brown sugar in a food processor for 5 minutes it turns pale golden. Add the eggs and process to combine. Add the flour and process until smooth. Turn the pastry onto a lightly floured surface and roll out into a round flat disc. Wrap this in clingfilm and refrigerate for 2 hours. Preheat oven to 180°C. Roll pastry onto a lightly floured surface to 2mm thick and separate it to line six 75mm diameter by 40mm deep pie pans. Trim edges and refrigerate for 30 minutes. Bake blind for 10 minutes or until crisp and golden. Cool for 5 minutes in the pans, then remove pastry shells from pans and place on a baking tray.

Italian meringue
Combine caster sugars and water in a heavy-bottomed saucepan over low heat and stir until sugar dissolves. Increase heat until almost boiling (if you have a sugar thermometer, to 115°C) and remove from the heat. Using an electric mixer, whisk the egg whites in a bowl until they form soft peaks. Continuing to whisk, slowly add the hot syrup, then keep whisking for 5 minutes.

WINE: Stony Brook Annie's Wine 2003 – peach and apricot notes with floral undertones

Serves 8

450g puff pastry dough
4 tablespoons melted butter
4 tablespoons brown sugar
4 Granny Smith or Golden Delicious apples
8 tablespoons cold unsalted butter
Cinnamon sugar, to garnish
8 mint sprigs, to garnish
2 cups vanilla ice cream

Apple tart *fine*

Roll out the puff pastry dough and prick it all over with a fork. Using a dish or circular stencil 40mm in diameter, cut 8 discs out of the dough. Place pastry discs on a baking tray and leave to stand for 15 minutes. Preheat the oven to 200°C. Brush each disc with melted butter and sprinkle with brown sugar. Peel, halve, and core the apples, then slice finely. Arrange apple slices in a rosette design on each pastry disc. Brush the tops of the apple slices with melted butter, sprinkle with brown sugar and place a tablespoon of cold butter in the centre of each tart. Bake the tarts at 200°C for 20–30 minutes. The dough will rise slightly and the apples will begin to caramelise. Serve sprinkled with cinnamon sugar, garnished with mint sprigs and with scoops of vanilla ice cream on the side.

WINE: Delheim Edelspatz Noble Late Harvest 2007 – pineapple-flavoured richness, lifted by arresting acidity

Makes 15

15 wooden chopsticks or paddle-pop sticks
15 small Red Delicious or Pink Lady apples, washed and dried
4 cups white sugar
1 cup water
½ teaspoon cream of tartar
2 teaspoons red liquid food colouring

Cinnamon custard
1 cup milk
2 cups pouring cream
1 cinnamon stick
8 egg yolks
150g caster sugar

Toffee apples with cinnamon custard

Push a stick into each apple. Line two baking trays with baking paper. Heat the sugar and water in a heavy-bottomed saucepan over low heat. Simmer, stirring continuously, until the sugar has dissolved completely. Stop stirring and increase heat until the syrup boils. Using a wet pastry brush, brush away any sugar crystals that have stuck to the sides of the saucepan above the syrup level. Stir in the cream of tartar and food colouring. Reduce heat to low. Simmer the toffee for 20 minutes or until it reaches hard, cracking stage. (To check if it has reached this stage, add 1 teaspoon of toffee to a glass of ice-cold water. Remove solidified toffee from the cold water and bend it. The toffee should crack easily and not bend or feel sticky.) Once toffee is at this stage, remove from heat immediately. Wait until toffee stops bubbling, then dip one apple into the toffee. Tip the pan at an angle to coat it completely, especially around the base of the stick. Place coated toffee apple onto the prepared baking tray. Repeat with remaining apples and leave to set at room temperature. Serve with cinnamon custard.

Cinnamon custard
Bring the milk, cream and cinnamon stick to simmering point in a heavy-bottomed saucepan over low heat. Whisk the egg yolks and caster sugar in a heatproof bowl until pale and creamy. Whisk the hot cinnamon-milk mixture into the egg mixture to incorporate. Stand the bowl over a pan of gently simmering water and stir until the custard thickens. Remove the bowl from the heat and push the custard through a fine sieve into a clean heatproof bowl. Discard the cinnamon stick. Serve immediately or cover with clingwrap and refrigerate. Reheat over a pan of simmering water, whisking to keep it smooth.

WINE: Simonsig Vin de Liza Noble Late Harvest 2006 – apricot earthy tones, minerally rich

Boeber with vanilla-rum banana

Serves 6

500g tapioca, soaked overnight in water
2 litres milk
2 cups sugar
About 1 teaspoon ground cinnamon, to taste
250g butter
2 tablespoons caster sugar
2 bananas, peeled and sliced
Seeds scraped from 1 moist, fresh vanilla pod
1/4 cup Bacardi rum

The first thing I ever learnt to cook, while helping my mother in the kitchen for our traditional Sunday lunch, was custard. I have always had a sweet tooth, so this is where my first interests lay. From there I moved on to my favourite childhood pudding, boeber. *This is a tapioca pudding with milk and cinnamon, one of the world's most comforting dishes.*

Add tapioca to milk and bring to the boil. Add sugar, cinnamon and butter and cook over low heat, stirring continuously. Cook slowly for 15–20 minutes, until the mixture starts to thicken and the tapioca is cooked through. In a nonstick frying pan, heat the caster sugar until it caramelises lightly. Add the banana slices, vanilla seeds and rum, carefully set the rum alight and flambé the bananas until well caramelised. To serve, spoon the tapioca into serving bowls and top with vanilla-rum banana slices.

WINE: Swartland Red Jerepigo – bursting with delicious fruit-pastille aromas, well-balanced and fresh

pestle and mortar

(stocks, pastes and sauces)

Master stock

Makes 2 cups

- 1 cup water
- 2 cups chicken stock
- 3 cinnamon sticks
- 1/2 cup brown sugar
- 50g piece fresh ginger, roughly chopped
- Zest of 1/2 orange
- 1/2 cup Kikkoman soy sauce
- 2 whole star anise

I didn't have a classical chef's training – I learnt as I went along – so it took me a while to understand soups, stocks and reducing. It's quite simple in concept but hard to get right. The flavour and the consistency have to arrive at the same time. If the flavour is right but the stock is too liquid, you will make the flavour too strong by reducing. Likewise, if the consistency is right but the flavour isn't there yet, you'll ruin the consistency by further reduction. It's something you learn to feel as you go along.

Combine all the ingredients in a large pot and bring to the boil. Reduce heat and simmer for 4–5 minutes. Remove from the heat and leave to cool. When cooled completely, strain and refrigerate until ready to use.

Lamb broth

Makes about 3 litres

- 1kg lamb bones
- 500g chicken wings
- 2 onions, peeled and coarsely chopped
- 4 carrots, peeled and coarsely chopped
- 5 stalks celery, coarsely chopped
- 2 stalks flat-leaf parsley
- 2 sprigs thyme
- 1 tablespoon whole black peppercorns
- 4 litres cold water
- Sea salt

The broth freezes well for later use.

Preheat oven to 220°C. Place lamb bones and chicken wings in a large roasting pan and roast for 30 minutes or until dark brown in colour. Combine bones and wings in a large saucepan with all the remaining ingredients except the salt. Bring to the boil, then reduce heat to medium and simmer for 3 hours, occasionally skimming the fat off the surface. Season to taste. Strain through a fine sieve, reserving the stock and discarding solids.

Veal stock reduction

Makes 3 litres

4½kg veal bones
2 carrots, coarsely chopped
2 stalks celery, coarsely chopped
1 yellow onion, coarsely chopped
1 leek, cleaned and coarsely chopped
1 whole bulb garlic, cut in half crosswise
2 tablespoons canola oil
½ cup skinned, seeded and chopped tomato
4 cups dry red wine
8 litres cold water

Preheat the oven to 110°C. Place the veal bones in a roasting pan and roast in the oven for about 2 hours or until golden brown. When bones are done, place the carrots, celery, onion, leek, garlic and canola oil in a large stockpot. Cook over a medium heat, stirring, until caramelised. Add the tomato and cook for 5 minutes. Deglaze with the red wine and reduce until most of the wine has evaporated. Add the browned bones and cover with cold water. Bring to the boil, then reduce heat and simmer over medium heat for 8 hours. Strain into a fresh pot through a fine sieve. Discard the solids and simmer the remaining liquid over medium heat for 45 minutes or until it coats the back of a spoon. Reduction can be used immediately or stored in the freezer for several months.

Basil pesto

Makes 200g

15g pine nuts
1 clove garlic, peeled and chopped
60g basil leaves, stalks removed
100ml extra virgin olive oil
20g grated Parmesan cheese, preferably Reggiano
Salt and black pepper

Toast the pine nuts in a dry frying pan over medium heat until golden brown – watch them carefully as this will only take a few minutes. Place the garlic and pine nuts in a food processor and blend until smooth. Add the basil leaves, and gradually add the olive oil, pulsing to form a green paste. Add the grated Parmesan, blend for 10–15 seconds and season with salt and pepper to taste.

Red wine jus

Makes 6 litres

20 tablespoons canola oil
10 cups chopped Spanish onion
10 cups chopped carrot
1 cup chopped celery
10 Granny Smith apples, cored and cut into eighths
4 x 750ml bottles red wine
3 x 750ml bottles port
10 litres beef stock

Heat the canola oil in a large pot and fry the onion, carrot, celery and apple over high heat for 15 minutes, or until golden-brown and caramelised. Add red wine and port and cook until reduced by half. Add stock and cook until jus reaches syrup consistency. Strain, cool and keep in the fridge until needed (it also freezes well).

REUBEN'S SUPPLIER LIST

Adelaarsvlug (fresh herbs)	021 863 1231
Atlas Trading (dry spices)	021 423 4361
Basic Foods (dry goods)	021 872 0319
Chalmar beef (red meat)	021 951 3169
CNC Products (nuts)	021 552 4212
Fine Huguenot Chocolates (chocolate)	021 876 4096
Franschhoek Olive Oil Company	021 876 3243
Gastrofoods (pork, guinea fowl, duck, calves' liver)	021 951 3169
Get Stuffed Enterprises (cheese)	021 448 8063
Goede Hoop Butchery (lamb)	021 863 2965
Gordon's Bay Fisheries (fresh fish, seafood)	021 856 3686
Joostenberg (pork)	021 884 4208
Malan Dairy (butter, milk, cream)	021 872 8868
Roubaix Fresh Produce (fruit and vegetables)	021 876 3470
Sue Baker, Wild Peacock Products (quails, chorizo, wild peacock)	021 865 2380
Three Streams (salmon, salmon trout, squid)	021 876 2485
Truckles (cheese)	021 876 4928

REUBEN'S
UNDER THE SKIN OF SA'S BEST RESTAURANT

One of the things that has stayed with me from my time at Chamonix, my first restaurant job, is how the staff were treated and the unity there was among us. We worked hard and our chef was strict, but every day we all sat down together and had an excellent meal. If you want caring, personal service in a restaurant, you have to treat your staff in a caring, personal way.

Christophe Dehosse, my first mentor, taught me that discipline can be achieved without screaming and shouting, and without belittling people. Respect comes naturally when everyone knows what is important – the food.

Running a good restaurant means knowing what sort of staff to hire. You need a certain type of person, and this is not dependent on qualifications – I have worked with people who trained under Gordon Ramsay, and some were good but some were shocking in the kitchen. Restaurant workers need drive, dedication and commitment, but I don't believe in running a regimented, task-only kitchen. You have to know people, and care for them, to get the best food on tables.

I employ many family members, and as far as possible, only people from the Franschhoek valley. This adds to the restaurant's regional flavour and also helps me feel as though I'm giving something back to the community that raised me. Not all these people are trained when they come to Reuben's, but they all have an understanding of what is required and a sense of loyalty.

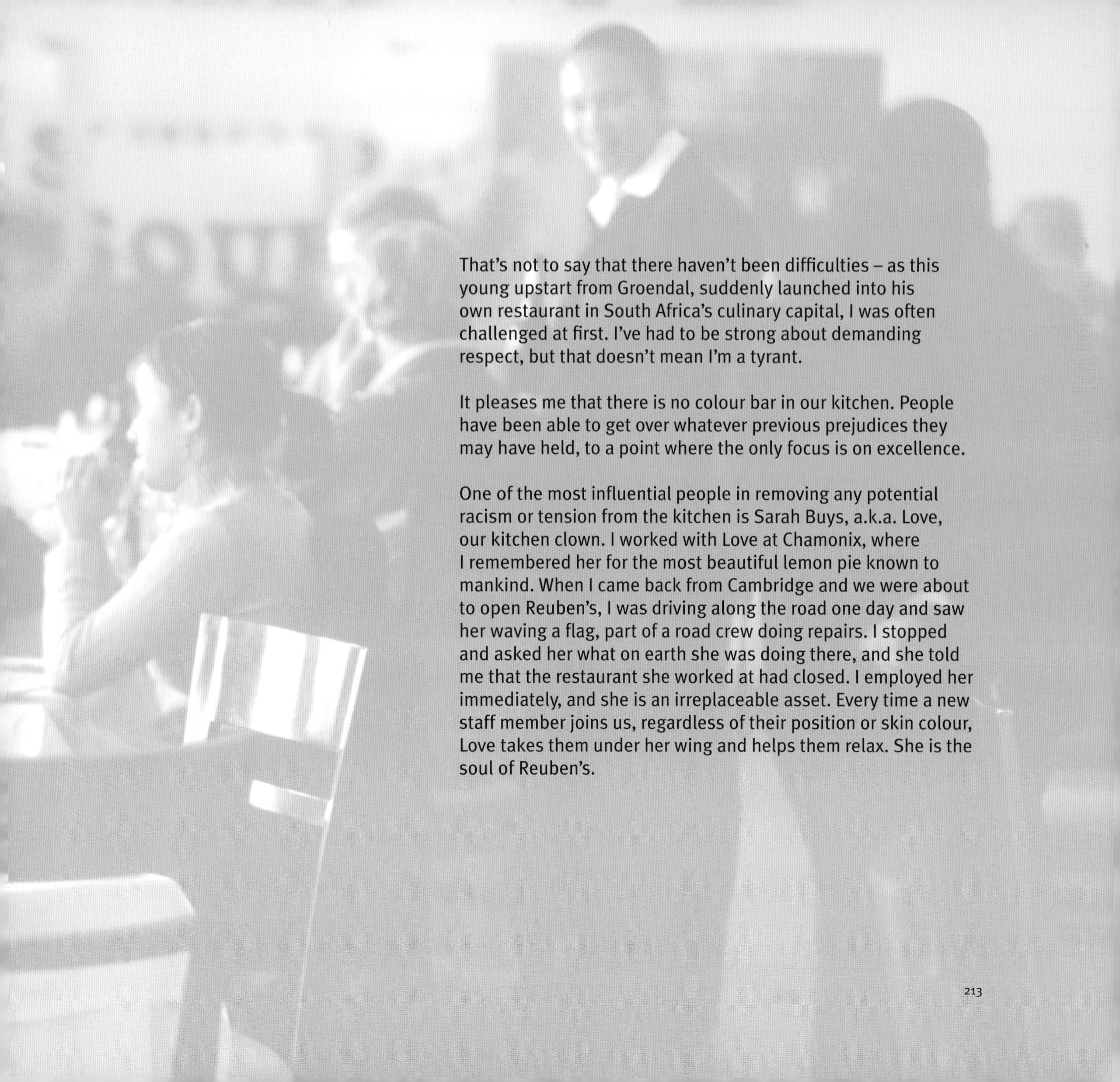

That's not to say that there haven't been difficulties – as this young upstart from Groendal, suddenly launched into his own restaurant in South Africa's culinary capital, I was often challenged at first. I've had to be strong about demanding respect, but that doesn't mean I'm a tyrant.

It pleases me that there is no colour bar in our kitchen. People have been able to get over whatever previous prejudices they may have held, to a point where the only focus is on excellence.

One of the most influential people in removing any potential racism or tension from the kitchen is Sarah Buys, a.k.a. Love, our kitchen clown. I worked with Love at Chamonix, where I remembered her for the most beautiful lemon pie known to mankind. When I came back from Cambridge and we were about to open Reuben's, I was driving along the road one day and saw her waving a flag, part of a road crew doing repairs. I stopped and asked her what on earth she was doing there, and she told me that the restaurant she worked at had closed. I employed her immediately, and she is an irreplaceable asset. Every time a new staff member joins us, regardless of their position or skin colour, Love takes them under her wing and helps them relax. She is the soul of Reuben's.

REUBEN'S SUPPLIER LIST

Adelaarsvlug (fresh herbs)	021 863 1231
Atlas Trading (dry spices)	021 423 4361
Basic Foods (dry goods)	021 872 0319
Chalmar beef (red meat)	021 951 3169
CNC Products (nuts)	021 552 4212
Fine Huguenot Chocolates (chocolate)	021 876 4096
Franschhoek Olive Oil Company	021 876 3243
Gastrofoods (pork, guinea fowl, duck, calves' liver)	021 951 3169
Get Stuffed Enterprises (cheese)	021 448 8063
Goede Hoop Butchery (lamb)	021 863 2965
Gordon's Bay Fisheries (fresh fish, seafood)	021 856 3686
Joostenberg (pork)	021 884 4208
Malan Dairy (butter, milk, cream)	021 872 8868
Roubaix Fresh Produce (fruit and vegetables)	021 876 3470
Sue Baker, Wild Peacock Products (quails, chorizo, wild peacock)	021 865 2380
Three Streams (salmon, salmon trout, squid)	021 876 2485
Truckles (cheese)	021 876 4928

CONVERSION CHARTS

All measurements in cups, tablespoons and teaspoons used throughout are level measures
All chicken is free-range
All eggs are free-range and organic, so may vary in size, but use large wherever possible
Anything cooked or baked in the oven is on the middle shelf unless otherwise stated

Liquids

Metric	Standard	Imperial
5ml	1 teaspoon	3/16 fl oz
15ml	1 tablespoon	1/2 fl oz
60ml	1/4 cup (4 tablespoons)	2 fl oz
80ml	1/3 cup	2 2/3 fl oz
125ml	1/2 cup	4 1/2 fl oz
160ml	2/3 cup	5 1/2 fl oz
180ml	3/4 cup	7 fl oz
250ml	1 cup	9 fl oz

Oven temperatures

Celsius	Fahrenheit	Gas mark	Description
100°C	200°F	1/4	Cool
110°C	225°F	1/4	Cool
120°C	250°F	1/2	Very low
140°C	275°F	1	Very low
150°C	300°F	2	Low
160°C	325°F	3	Low
180°C	350°F	4	Moderate
190°C	375°F	5	Moderate
200°C	400°F	6	Moderate-high
220°C	425°F	7	High
230°C	450°F	8	High
240°C	475°F	9	Very high

RECIPES REUBEN RIFFEL | **WORDS** SUE DE GROOT
PHOTOGRAPHS CRAIG FRASER | **DESIGN & PRODUCTION** LIBBY DOYLE
DTP ANDREA WILLMORE | **COPY EDITOR** ROBYN ALEXANDER

ALL PROPS WITH THANKS TO
MARTI FOSTER OF **MASQUERADE** 021 876 3944
ANDRÉ CROUSE OF **PLUSH BAZAAR** 021 447 6495
TINA BESTER OF **QUEEN OF TARTS** 021 448 2420

This edition is the second printing of *Reuben Cooks: Food is Time Travel*

ALSO AVAILABLE IN AFRIKAANS

FIRST PUBLISHED IN 2008 BY QUIVERTREE PUBLICATIONS
PO Box 51051 • Waterfront • 8002 • Cape Town • South Africa
T: +27 (0) 21 461 6808 • F: +27 (0) 21 461 6842 • E: info@quivertree.co.za
www.quivertree.co.za

DISTRIBUTED BY QUIVERTREE PUBLICATIONS
PO Box 51051 • Waterfront • 8002 • Cape Town • South Africa
T: +27 (0) 21 461 6808 • F: +27 (0) 21 461 6842 • E: info@quivertree.co.za

ISBN: 978-0-9802651-5-6

QUIVERTREE PUBLICATIONS, PLACES GREAT VALUE ON THE ENVIRONMENT AND IS ACTIVELY INVOLVED IN EFFORTS TO PRESERVE IT. THE PAPER USED IN THE PRODUCTION OF THIS BOOK WAS SUPPLIED BY MILLS THAT SOURCE THEIR RAW MATERIALS FROM SUSTAINABLY MANAGED FORESTS. SOY-BASED INKS WERE USED IN ITS PRINTING.

A NOTE ON PHOTOGRAPHY

Craig Fraser has been photographing food for the last decade. He has illustrated several cookbooks and worked for many of the major magazines as well as prestigious commercial food clients. *Feast* by Franck Dangereux and *Lazy Days* by Phillippa Cheifitz (both published by Quivertree) were both illustrated by Craig, and both won their respective categories at the prestigious Gourmand World Cookbook Awards. He also recently produced the photographs for one of Quivertree's latest titles, *Prickly Pears and Pomegranates* by Bernadette le Roux and Marianne Palmer. Craig believes that food is one of the great pleasures of life, and the photographs in this book vividly convey his passion for food to the reader.

TECHNICAL INFORMATION ON PHOTOGRAPHY

Photographs for this book were all taken on location and only 'available light' was used. The photographer used a Hasselblad 6cm x 6cm format camera for the food photographs, and a Nikon F5 35mm camera for the scenery and mood pictures. Everything was photographed on Fuji Provia 100asa film.

D

E

F

G

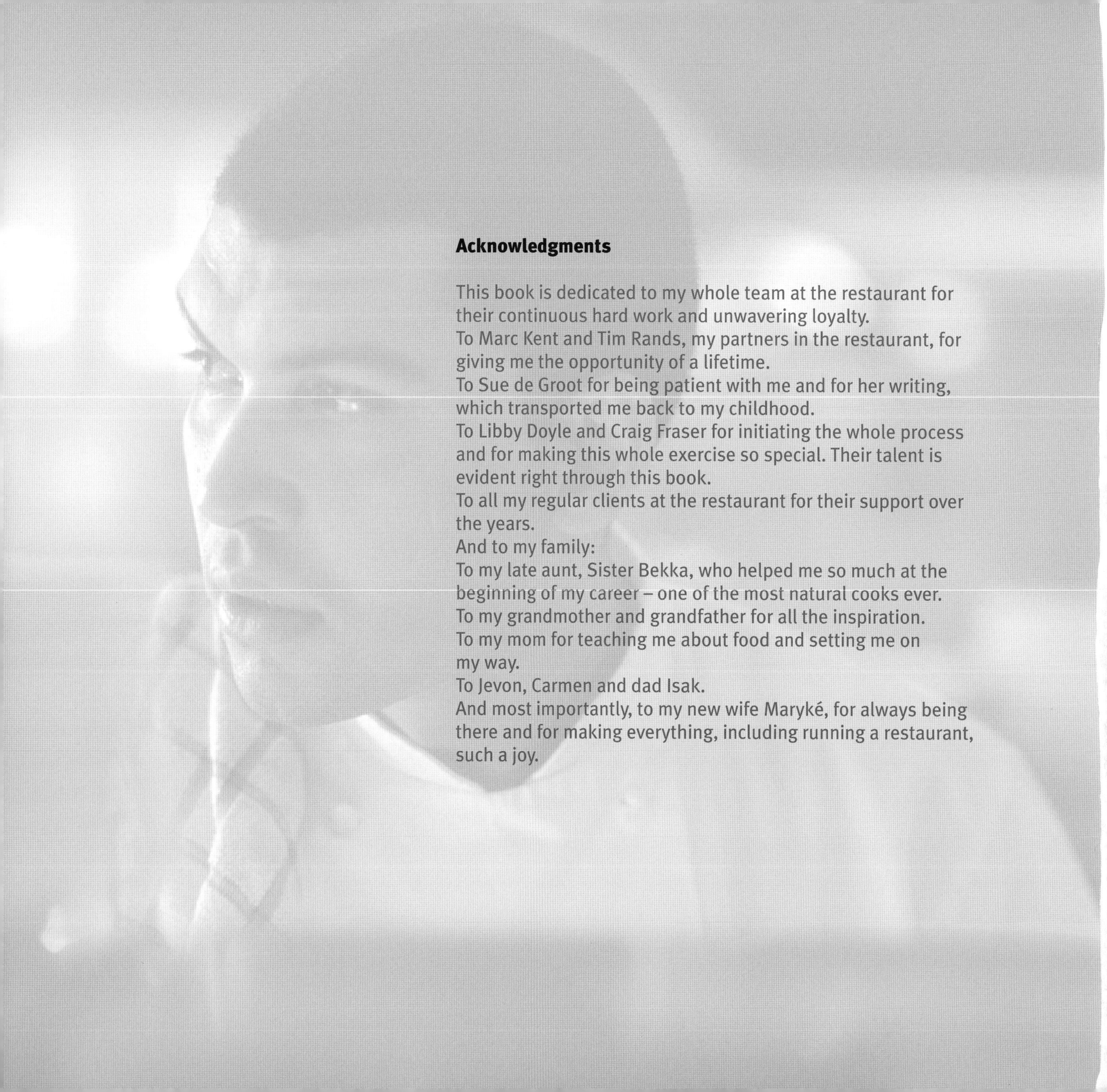

Acknowledgments

This book is dedicated to my whole team at the restaurant for their continuous hard work and unwavering loyalty.
To Marc Kent and Tim Rands, my partners in the restaurant, for giving me the opportunity of a lifetime.
To Sue de Groot for being patient with me and for her writing, which transported me back to my childhood.
To Libby Doyle and Craig Fraser for initiating the whole process and for making this whole exercise so special. Their talent is evident right through this book.
To all my regular clients at the restaurant for their support over the years.
And to my family:
To my late aunt, Sister Bekka, who helped me so much at the beginning of my career – one of the most natural cooks ever.
To my grandmother and grandfather for all the inspiration.
To my mom for teaching me about food and setting me on my way.
To Jevon, Carmen and dad Isak.
And most importantly, to my new wife Maryké, for always being there and for making everything, including running a restaurant, such a joy.